TEACH ME!

TEACH ME!

KIDS WILL LEARN WHEN OPPRESSION IS THE LESSON
Expanded Edition

Murray Levin

ROWMAN & LITTLEFIELD PUBLISHERS, INC.
Lanham • Boulder • New York • Oxford

Publication of this book is made possible by The Judy Ruben Outreach Fund.

ROWMAN & LITTLEFIELD PUBLISHERS, INC.

Published in the United States of America
by Rowman & Littlefield Publishers, Inc.
4720 Boston Way, Lanham, Maryland 20706
http://www.rowmanlittlefield.com

12 Hid's Copse Road, Cumnor Hill, Oxford OX2 9JJ, England

British Library Cataloguing in Publication Information Available

Library of Congress Cataloging-in-Publication Data

Levin, Murray Burton.
    Teach me! : kids will learn when oppression is the lesson / Murray
Levin.—Expanded ed.
       p. cm.
    ISBN 0-7425-0174-4 (pbk. : alk. paper)
       1. Education, Urban—United States—Case studies.   2. Afro-Americans—
Education (Secondary)—Case studies.   3. Hispanic Americans—Education
(Secondary)—Case studies.   4. Socially handicapped youth—Education
(Secondary)—United States—Case studies.   5. Greater Egleston Community High
School (Boston, Mass.).   I. Title.

LC5131 .L44   2001
373.1829'96073—dc21

                                                                    00-059198

Printed in the United States of America

∞™ The paper used in this publication meets the minimum requirements of American
National Standard for Information Sciences—Permanence of Paper for Printed Library
Materials, ANSI/NISO Z39.48-1992.

To Beatriz, Terri, Ken, and Billy,
who gave life and hope to so many

CONTENTS

A C K N O W L E D G M E N T S

෴

My students at Egleston taught me about survival and courage, as well as about how it is possible to learn under harsh and hateful conditions and still fulfill dreams. I honor and thank them.

Computers and word processing were developed long after I became addicted to fountain pens, so I thank Carlos Suarez, Joshua and Judith Shapiro, and Danielle Michelin, who transcribed dozens of tapes and drafts of this book.

Many friends and colleagues, including Joseph Boskin, Andrew Cohn, Ann Coolidge, Herbert Englehart, Gladys Topkis, and my wife Helen Jacobson, helped me clarify my thoughts and taught me that shorter is better. I want to acknowledge my debt to Elizabeth Mayer who edited *Teach Me!* with so much intelligence and grace.

I cannot forget Judith Ruben who brought this book to Monthly Review Press. A loving and joyous friend, wise, warm, and political, she understood.

∾

"They Put Us in a Brown Bag and Shake Us"

The Greater Egleston Community High School is a venue of last resort, the ultimate way station of some Boston schools that have become holding pens to keep the students unarmed, uneducated, and off the streets until midafternoon. In 1993, after forty-five years of teaching political theory at Columbia College, Boston University, Stonehill College, and the Harvard Extension School, I began to teach a course at Egleston, located in Jamaica Plain, in one of Boston's more dilapidated ghettos. Egleston has about seventy students, evenly distributed between blacks and Latinos, boys and girls, many of whom are dropouts and discards. I spent three years at the school, teaching, tutoring, counseling, acting as an employment agency, lending a solicitous hand and a few dollars, listening, and grieving with students who lost friends in the senseless slaughter of gang wars and drive-by shootings, where a step to the left or right or a minute earlier or later would have meant a life saved.

I had to teach kids who were cast out, kids whose lives might be altered by a bit of attention and innovative instruction. I was no longer teaching only privileged college kids on their way to business or law school, where they would learn how to facilitate the flow of corporate capital.

My friends worried about my safety. Two friends, distinguished African-American historians, urged me not to go because I didn't understand where I was going. They urged me to ask the school for safe transportation and proposed that I get a black driver. One gave me a list of twenty books to read (I didn't); the other suggested that I read *The Invisible Man*, wear work clothes, and buy a portable phone.

I did not intend to write a book about the kids or the ghetto or the pedagogy or anything connected with Egleston. I have lived through the pain and pleasure of writing several books, and I knew the bondage that writing bestows upon authors. I went to teach and feel useful, although I knew practically nothing about black or Latino culture, and I had never taught in a high school.

During my third week at Egleston, I joined three students who were talking about how the government developed the AIDS virus to infect and kill blacks and Latinos. They spoke of other conspiracies—how the U.S. government promoted the importation of heroin and cocaine, which it then distributed to ghettos at great profit. These theories were designed to explain the students' powerlessness, but their world view was more complex. The government was also part of a grand conspiracy that brought together the president and congressional leaders with drug lords and the heads of large corporations who sought to preserve the ghetto because it provided an endless supply of cheap labor and custom- ers for the cheap products, drugs, and cigarettes. Urban and suburban school systems, the students argued, supplemented this conspiracy by ensuring that middle-class whites would be well educated and blacks poorly educated. Good teachers were sent to the suburbs; racist and incompetent teachers were sent to the city. The bit of "reality" that "validated" these theories was local. According to these kids, police conspired to keep the ghetto as it was so they could continue to rob dealers and sell their drugs while collecting bribes to avoid streets where heavy drug traffic occurred. The local police became the model for a grand conspiracy. The fact that dealers prosper and multiply was proof that the state and business conspired to promote the drug trade.

I asked few questions during the two hours we were together. The kids talked about the American dream as a come-on designed to keep minorities committed to the system. They were acutely aware of white power and their own powerlessness. Felicia, the girl in the triad, described the bondage of the ghetto: "They put us in a brown bag and shake us." The students' alienation was profound. For them, the state was an oligarchy; elections were a cruel joke. The talk was paranoid, conspiratorial, apocalyptic, fascinating, but not entirely mad.

I have written extensively about alienated voters and the paranoid style in American politics, so I know the lament of the powerless. I decided to write an article about this astonishing conversation and to deal with these views as seriously as if they were the core ideology of a movement. The conspiratorial theme recurs periodically in American history because it is simple and unambiguous and accounts for the loss of power or status or the anxiety induced by massive change. For Egleston kids, the theory also involves the pleasure of casting the white man as a devil.

The article I envisioned has become a book—not about how black and Latino kids live, not about the lack of parenting or the sex life of these kids, not about the war of all against all waged in the ghetto. Although *Teach Me!* touches on all of these, it is an intellectual history, an analysis of how black and Latino adolescents see the world. It is an account of their political and social theory, their perception, their cognition, their despair, and their attraction to conspiratorial thinking. It is an account of their politics, their apoliticality, and their transcendent dreams.

A rich intellectual history is there, but this is also a book of invention, a record of new ways of teaching that dramatically changed the thinking of some troubled kids. This is a book that describes the evolution of a new and successful pedagogy that can be used in any school where teachers are willing. *Teach Me!* is not just a description of ghetto life. It is a prescription for change in urban education.

It was obvious to me soon after arriving at Egleston that my traditional teaching—read the text, analyze the text, discuss the text—would not work. It was also painfully obvious that many Egleston kids were not thinking clearly. They could remember specifics, but had trouble discriminating between the trivial and the important. Their thinking was episodic and fragmented, as if they created freeze frames in their mind, contextless snapshots beyond which everything was out of focus. Many had trouble thinking abstractly because they were wedded to a simple and brute empiricism.

During my first year, I assigned Howard Zinn's *A People's History of the United States*, a sympathetic history of the underclass that I thought would appeal to our class. Not one of my ten students could or would read a twenty-page chapter each week. I assigned parts of chapters, then xeroxed pages, then paragraphs, and finally summaries. The kids found the book boring and irrelevant.

But there were brilliant insights, short-lived phenomena like shooting stars, that suddenly lit the sky and quickly disappeared. The kids had trouble reading books and categorizing information, but they wrote beautiful poetry and imaginative short stories, and many became adept at the computer. Their subtlety was obvious when they described the strategies they employed to beat heavy Darwinian odds.

I decided to teach my students how to think clearly rather than give a standard course in American politics. We learned logic and a methodology for the social sciences. We studied how to identify a cause and an effect, how to analyze a system in terms of function and need, suppliers and consumers. We learned how and why conflict and opposition produce change. We talked about unintended consequences and learned a bit about game theory. We struggled over what constitutes a class and the role of class conflict. We even examined the state of our own class consciousness. We studied how politicians use anxiety to manipulate voters and how advertisers use sexual symbolism to win consumers. And we explored the relationship between the population of a nation and its predisposition for war. We spent three years studying this eccentric curriculum, which I assume is profoundly different from the plan of study used by most high schools.

I decided to teach logic and dialectics to these kids, and treat them as if they were graduate students. I abandoned textbooks. I used only primary sources. I assigned only large issues, cataclysmic events like the Cuban missile crisis, or seemingly less significant moments that nevertheless release profound human sentiments. For us, every project had to be relevant to daily life in some important way. We never dealt with problems that were so abstract and distant from us that we could not feel their meaning. We scrutinized how George Bush used the release of prisoner Willie Horton to frighten voters. We examined who profits from the ghetto. We dealt with the Cuban missile crisis in part because it was a potentially apocalyptic war, an enormous and grotesque version of war in the hood. We examined Kennedy's and Khrushchev's options as we would our own. We explicated texts as graduate students do, and we role-played as grammar school students do.

I always taught that thought is a weapon more powerful than any other they might possess. I tried to provide our class with a "Greek" education based on dialectics. We thought in terms of process, conflict, and resolution. In retrospect, I have realized that one of the most significant things we did was having lunch together. It was there that we unburdened ourselves and created the bond that transformed our class into a community.

The kids I taught live in the other America, where babies die younger and poverty is pervasive, where unwed mothers count more on government largesse than on a male provider. This is the other America you and I read about in college years ago, but now it is more primitive and more dangerous. *Teach Me!* is an oral history of who lives and who dies at Egleston, a verbatim recollection of the painful and often heroic effort to sit still, learn to read and write, and dream of building bridges. It is also about the refusal to learn.

Many of the girls have children. Many felt encumbered, chained to routines initiated by an instant of desire and a boyfriend who has long since disappeared. We have some brilliant kids at Egleston whose star is dimmed by depression or low self-esteem. We have crack dealers, car thieves, alcoholics, kids who work long hours to help their parents, kids who cannot do algebra but write elegant poetry, kids who read with difficulty but write belligerent, mournful, and arresting prose. We have kids who want to be architects, sound engineers, state troopers, nurses, grocery store owners, and physical therapists. Many of these young people will be consumed by violence and anomie long before they have a chance to realize themselves. But Egleston is also a second chance to live, a haven for kids whose life force has survived the urban holocaust.

During my three years at Egleston, I compiled an oral history of students, teachers, administrators, social workers, policemen, and community workers. *Teach Me!* is based on this rich and unique archive, a record of sadness and pathology and of the small steps that change lives. The quotations in this book, with rare exceptions, were taken from tape-recorded interviews with students or taped class sessions. When taping was impossible, I took notes and verified their contents with the students. I have changed all the names of the students and teachers who appear in this book, except for those whose poetry is quoted.

Teach Me! is about social decay, a marker for the malignancy of our time. It is about depression and mania and the abuse and cruelty imposed on a youthful underclass. It is about grief turned into melancholy and the love and rejection by mothers of their fatherless children.

Egleston was also for me a chance for rebirth at age seventy, a chance to search for new ways to reach kids who have abandoned all interest in learning. I spoke to kids who were high and kids who were drunk, kids who yearned for their missing father and others who wished he were dead. I spoke to kids who were nourished by parents and kids who had been man-of-the-house since age twelve or thirteen. I talked to a girl who surrendered a lucrative life selling cocaine to become a serious student. I spoke to a boy who described his girlfriend as "a rose, the flower who saved my life." I spoke to kids who read with difficulty and kids who wrote poignant short stories and elegiac poetry. Their stories and creativity in class taught me much, even as I instructed them.

༄

"Shit, Man, Teach Me": The Lament of the Forgotten

No matter what happens you can't get the truth. You can't find what's real. The government lies. People with power lie. This gives them power. They don't educate us. They put money into jails, not schools. I want to learn about Puerto Rican people, and they teach me white history. Fuck it. I don't know who I am, and that's what they want. It's like you got no past, no guides. You are a fucking orphan. It's like being blind. You can't see any heroes; we call them role models.

When I began my teaching, I had no idea who the students at the Greater Egleston Community High School were or what they expected. I had no idea what it meant to have no father or fear gang retribution or be hooked on dope or be too anxious and disoriented to read a book or join coequally in a lasting love. I never knew a ghetto kid—black or Latino—before I came to Egleston. I was in a foreign country—foreign food, foreign clothes, foreign norms. I had become the outsider, the alien, the weird one, white in a black and Latino world.

Yet it soon became clear to me that the students at this high school operated intellectually at the sixth- or seventh-grade level. None had a serious grasp of geography or history. Many read with difficulty. Very few could compose a literate paragraph, and very few ever read a book outside of school. I found myself getting angry at kids who said they couldn't study because they had no family, no father, or an alcoholic mother. I was so naive when I came to Egleston that I thought it would be easy to transcend such circumstances. I did not understand the power of the streets or the grieving for murdered friends or all the medication needed to soften the blow. I thought that you went to high school, studied hard, let nothing interfere, and went to college. I did not know at first that the culture of these kids was sensate, verbal, tactile, and melodic—but not literary. Theirs was a culture of style and dash and blazing light, a culture that had lost its past, believed in no future, and lived for the present. I realized none of this during my initiation, so I blamed the kids and yelled as if they were isolated atoms of free will.

I could not stand the fact that my students were disruptive and uninterested. It never occurred to me that I had anything to do with it. Their inability to read ten or twenty pages of a radical history each week increased my distance from them and my disdain. Instead of trying to understand who they were, I began to remove myself from their world as my disrespect grew.

But there was something in me that would not let me leave. I felt completely out of place, puzzled by what impulse drove me to teach ghetto kids. I know it had something to do with being Jewish, feeling guilty, loving learning, and sensing some identity, abstract at first, with potential victims of an unofficial but de facto apartheid.

My decision to work in the ghetto also had something to do with my commitment to radical politics, a deep if gradually weakened conviction that qualitative change is possible. Egleston seemed like a perfect place to see if it was possible to turn lives around. I tentatively decided to teach my students how to think, how to discern causes and effects, how to identify a system, how to appreciate that conflict and opposition must precede change. This decision excited me and led me to introduce the kids to the meaning of class and class conflict, of exploitation and alienation. I kept telling myself that I was not trying to radicalize them, just teaching them how to think. But this was a lie, a convenient lie because it let me believe that I was abiding by some mythical teachers' code that separated school from life, classroom from politics. The fact is, however, that I taught these kids how to provoke social change. My purpose developed slowly. Months went by before I abandoned a traditional curriculum, and it was only the excitement of this experiment, as well as some kids I loved, that bound me to Egleston.

Long before I found my voice, I spent weeks observing one teacher lowering standards to meet the lowest common denominator. He managed, I thought, to reinforce their students' low sense of self-esteem while boring them with Mickey Mouse projects that had little relevance to their lives. The smart kids were bored; the less gifted seemed to be lost in some private world where the hazards of ghetto life were catalogued. This pettifogging simply reinforced my desire to teach kids that thought can be sensual, a pleasure, and a weapon for social change. It was as if I found my niche. The question was whether I could put my plans in place.

On Thursday mornings, for three years, I departed from Newton, Massachusetts, the Garden City, where many people spend more money in a year cultivating lawns than the kids at Egleston spend on food. I passed the great opulent houses of Commonwealth Avenue—Georgian colonials, occasional Spanish haciendas with no Latino residents but the maid, Tudors and Victorians occupied by surgeons in constant touch with their brokers. Commonwealth Avenue would courteously give way to Beacon Street and the parkway that borders fashionable Chestnut Hill with its shopping mall—the most successful in the United States per

square foot—and with its stores like Bloomingdale's and Brooks Brothers, temples of conspicuous consumption. Then, in the company of
white boys and girls being driven to school in dad's Lexus or Volvo, I
would come to the Brookline Municipal Golf Course, a bit of upper-class
socialism, framed by endless and identical ranch houses scrubbed white.

Then I would see a bit of West Roxbury, the last enclave of the
lace-curtain Irish who did not flee the city when their coreligionist, Judge
Garrity, ordered their children to sit next to black kids in school. I would
make rights and lefts through streets of 1880s-vintage three-deckers that
housed the Irishmen who built much of Boston and the Irish women
who served tea to Brahman masters. Finally, Egleston Square would
emerge. Each twenty-minute-trip was a lesson on social stratification, a
sobering reminder that the egalitarian myths perpetuated by civics
teachers have little foundation. The trip reminded me that the melting
pot was more a self-serving motto of patriots than a description of reality
because the neighborhoods I passed were largely Protestant or Jewish or
Catholic, Irish or Black or Latino, separate and unequal. My conserva-
tive university students never tired of intoning the upward saga of the
Jews, the Irish, the Italians, the Greeks, the Scandinavians, the Poles,
and the Russians—whose histories led them to conclude that there was
something defective about black and Latino genes. It did no good for
me to cite the grotesque legacy of slavery and poverty and to argue that
something special did exist in these cultures.

I often took a faster, more direct route to Egleston Square, down the
Massachusetts Turnpike to Columbus Avenue, the gateway to the
ghetto, a broad once-beautiful boulevard now echoing with empty
warehouses and factories expatriated to countries where owners can pay
labor seven cents a hour. The empty buildings and shabby houses reflect
the exodus in the 1950s of 170,000 Bostonians who could not tolerate
integration. Their departure made Boston more black, more Hispanic,
more segregated, and more impoverished. The exodus helped to create

the first American permanent ghettos, seemingly immune to the renova-
tion schemes of government or private enterprise. "There is nothing
temporary about inner-city ghettos," Witold Rybczynski writes. "Ghettos are as intrinsic to the identity of the United States as New England
villages, vast national parks, and leafy suburbs.... It's necessary to confront the incontrovertible fact of the ghetto, and to recognize its immen-
sity, its persuasiveness, and its longevity."

For three years on Thursday mornings during the school year, I drove
up Columbus Avenue and wondered what was stored in those giant
brick warehouses. Then I would arrive at Egleston Square, the vicinity
where my grandparents lived more than one hundred years ago, immi-
grant Jews who pushed carts and sold needles and notions until they
saved enough to begin the trip to solvency and the classic American
passage to the suburbs. I would park my car in the school parking lot;
or if that was full, I would be forced to park on the street where my car
thwarted intruders with a security alarm, a metaphor for my distrust and
anxiety for black and Latino kids. My anxiety was well-founded: the keys
to my car were stolen on the first day I taught and never returned. After
that day, I always took my fountain pen or jacket when I left a room. I
never carried much money. I felt cheap, even racist, but I remained
cautious. I loved many Egleston kids but did not trust them.

During my initiation at Egleston, I was anxious as I drove up
Columbus Avenue. My heart would beat as I saw my world disappear
in the rear view mirror, and with it my safety. I. M. Pei's miracle of glass,
the John Hancock Building, with its literal reproduction of sunset and
sunrise was no longer visible. Boston was gone. In its place was Egleston
Square—eight or nine blocks of buildings built in the 1880s or 1890s,
whose general dilapidation was poorly camouflaged by peeling coats of
paint. Many buildings had boarded windows and iron curtains waiting
to exclude unwelcome night shoppers. There were tiny storefront
churches promising salvation, check-cashing companies, and several

beauty parlors, some of which were minimultinationals that faxed, xeroxed, prepared tax returns, lent money, checked immigration papers, notorized, translated, and brokered real estate. There were several barber shops that served as communication headquarters for ghetto banter, a laundromat, stores that provided long-distance telephone calls and cabled money, and others that sold cellular phones and beepers. The square had two liquor stores that specialized in cheap booze and a private home that catered to those who needed alcohol after hours. Egleston Square was an emerging market, a highly competitive free enterprise zone, where drug pushers, storefront ministers, and liquor dealers catered, each in a different way, to the anxious, the lost and the impoverished.

Egleston Square, of course, is not unique. There are thousands of Egleston Squares in this country. Some are Latino, some are black. Some are large enough to support competitive markets that limit gouging. Some have honest cops who don't steal dope. A few have decent schools and support systems. They are all different, and they are mostly the same—rundown, dirty, and poor, everyone trying to play catch up while local factories leave and unemployment lines lengthen.

The economy of the ghetto flourishes because the poor have less but pay more. Merchants prosper by providing services for people who cannot afford the normal paraphernalia of the middle-class life: telephones, washers, dryers, savings, banks, lawyers, accountants, credit, domestic help. Some merchants price goods to meet welfare payments. The need to purchase and repurchase, pay and pay more, is the Gresham's law of the ghetto. Car lots and repair garages envelop both sides of Columbus Avenue. Car dealers peddle unreliable vehicles, four to eight years old, that sell for two to five thousand dollars. These soon provide an enviable feast for mechanics. The poor pay more to cash checks, borrow money, and acquire credit. Egleston girls, primarily Latino, have their hair and nails done frequently. The beauty parlors in the ghetto offer a magical kingdom that temporarily obliterates the mundane and transforms plain girls into princesses, sex queens, and wonder women who transcend the sorrow of the square.

The centerpiece of Egleston Square is the new and anomalous Fleet Bank, New England's financial colossus, that cohabits with another giant, its next-door neighbor, McDonald's. Fleet Bank, one of the many that once had little to do with blacks and Latinos, has not merely repented but has fallen in love with this community. It has placed a large billboard in the parking lot of the school that proclaims in large black letters *Estamos Aquí Para Egleston Square*. The other side announces in identical black letters *We're Here for Egleston Square—Fleet Bank*. The bank, McDonald's, and four new and well-designed stores (a pharmacy, a laundromat, a bakery, and a video rental) remind me of a Potemkin village, a Russian town made of scenery and facades, designed to impress foreign visitors and draw attention from drab and impoverished villages.

The Greater Egleston Community High School, located in the center of the square, is an unprepossessing brick and cement building, probably a converted warehouse or factory. Five classrooms are used for courses. Some have the original and attractive brick walls; others plaster facades covered with maps of South and Central America, portraits of Martin Luther King and Malcolm X, and Spanish and English phrases exhorting students to equal the accomplishments of their ancestors. Almost every window is covered by a screen to ensure that only our students will enjoy the pleasure of study. The school has four major subjects—English, math, history, and computer science—but students can also take yoga, painting, photography, newspaper, and parenting.

One half of the students are absent almost every day. Some are busy trying to curb the disorder of their families and the anarchy of their own lives. Some stay away because school seems to lead nowhere. Attendance often varies inversely with the weather. The New England fall and spring can be more seductive than the school. Years before I came to Egleston, students, extraordinary artists, covered the side wall of the school with a huge mural in the tradition of Orozco and Rivera. The mural expressed their defiance and willingness to resort to violence. Today it reminds our kids that hope always exists and the human spirit can overcome any obstacle. The mural may be formulaic, a compulsive rosary bead, but at least it reminds the students that a world exists beyond Egleston. Malcolm X and Martin Luther King, magnified beyond life, urge the students at Egleston to transcend traditional schooling: *Para Quintarnos la Patria, Primero Tienen Que Quitarnos La Vida* (To Take Away Our Faith, First You Have To Take Away Our Life). In larger letters is written, "The Violence Has Just Begun." The Reverend King reiterates, "I Have A Dream."

But very few dreams are fulfilled by the Egleston students or those in most inner-city schools. The desperation of these kids reflects the drastic changes that have occurred in urban America. The kids are in many ways victims of demography and shifting labor markets. American cities have always had skid rows, but today's ghettos are different: much larger, more segregated, and intractable. The population of two-thirds of the seventy-six largest cities in this country almost quadrupled between 1950 and 1990, but twenty-six cities lost one in every four citizens. Industry has relocated to the suburbs, the sunbelt, Mexico, and Asia. People and jobs have moved from large cities to small. The distribution of population within metropolitan areas has also changed drastically. Most of the jobs in metropolitan areas are now concentrated in suburbs where wealth is also concentrated. These shifts are unprecedented in urban history—so many great cities losing their economic vitality, culture, and population in such a rich and powerful county. The people who leave cities are usually middle class. The people who remain tend to be poor. The tax base declines. Social expenses increase. The social infrastructure collapses. Many downtown districts attract investment and new residents, but inner cities, crime ridden and impoverished, have drastically lost population.

The students at Egleston grew up in a city that prospers at the center and perishes at the periphery. More people visit Quincy Market in downtown Boston than they do Disney World. The city is a vast complex of skyscrapers, a financial, a legal, and an insurance center where mutual-fund managers in their thirties make one or two million dollars a year. By contrast, Greater Boston has lost eighty thousand jobs in the 1990s and approximately 20 percent of Boston citizens live in poverty. Almost one-third of the city, 30 percent to be exact, fell below the poverty line by 1985, and the great majority of the poor were black and Latino. The citywide youth unemployment rate was about 24 percent in the 1980s. According to the 1990 census, 47 percent of all Boston families with children are single-parent families. Sixty-five percent of black children and 78 percent of Latino children are born into single-parent families.

Boston is dominated by professional, technical, managerial, and service positions. Lack of education and skills therefore correlates with poverty. In 1985, 23 percent of the adults in Boston above age twenty-five lacked a high school diploma; in black and Latino neighborhoods, the figure is around 40 percent. Poverty spawns violence. So many buildings in Egleston Square are fortified bunkers, and increasing numbers of ghetto residents feel demoralized by the breakdown of social order. The ghetto is the land's end of social disintegration and therefore can only suffocate and confine. It is a prison without walls that has created a traditional society where little changes and life is governed by precedent, style, and scarcity.

Most of the deaths and much of the crime around Egleston Square are directly related to gang rivalry over turf and to drug trafficking. Gang life and culture profoundly affect life and death in the neighborhood. Although gangs are centered in housing projects, the whole Egleston neighborhood knows that gang members shift their allegiance, which disturbs the balance of power and exacerbates the struggle for turf and drugs.

The anomie and economic debilitation of Egleston Square is met by an army of social service agencies that attempt to alter the environment. This is an ancient American business. Since the time of Jefferson, Americans have firmly believed that knowledge and human nature are the products of sensations received from the external world. A new environment will produce a new array of sensations, which, in turn, will produce a new human nature. Americans are therefore massive manipulators of environment, architects of new housing projects, new schools, new welfare systems, new tax incentives, new approaches to social work, new ways of teaching, new enterprise zones, new housing projects, new community organizations, and new empowerment zones. Greater Egleston is enveloped by experiments designed to alter the environment and the flow of sensations, but the results are negligible. The dialectic between ghetto and agency is Hegelian. As it becomes increasingly obvious that the ghetto has become a permanent feature of urban America, agencies multiply and cry for funds, theories hyperventilate, and the statistics that calibrate social disintegration shriek calamity.

This is the world that Egleston students live in, a world where it is much easier to prosper in the illegal and underground economy than pursue a job at McDonald's or the laundry room of a hospital. If the past is prologue to the future, the kids at Egleston are lost, suspended in some time warp that has obliterated their past and mystified their future. These kids believe their history has been mutilated by teachers who glorify the white man's past. It is as if they were born yesterday, naked and childless, without ancestors or progeny. They are not unlike American Indians, severed from the myths and rhythms of their past, suspended in some arid plain. This is the Eglestonian liturgy, the primal scream: the past is lost—a powerless present and a hopeless future. The kids at Egleston have been robbed of their patrimony, a loss so great that only learned black men can restore the legends of African history.

One day during my second month at Egleston, when some students were still disdainful—silence in the hallway as I passed, a muted but nasty diffidence in class—two boys and a girl were talking in an empty classroom about why the ghetto was a prison. Robert, David, and Felicia became my first tutors. They initiated me into the nuances of conspiratorial theory and the laws that governed political economy. Much of what they told me was paranoid and ridiculous, but much was remarkably subtle and sophisticated.

Robert compared Roxbury to South Africa. Felicia wanted to know why white teachers distort black and Latino history. David agreed that the kids at Egleston don't know who they are because they have been robbed of their past. I introduced myself and asked if I might listen. They were uninterested but accepting. Later I asked if I could tape their conversation. No one objected—as a matter of fact, I felt they believed that the taping lent authenticity to their remarks. They began to feel that the record became official. They talked more slowly, paused more frequently, and began to point out the questions I overlooked.

Teachers don't know shit. The teachers that are going to be in the hood, the inner city, O.K., we won't teach them the right thing. We are going to lie to them. And the teachers in white communities, we're going to teach them the right way. It ain't even teachers. It goes higher. Congress sits there and be like O.K., teachers in Roxbury, we're going to teach them this.

You start with history. History is what somebody else is telling you. They're reading a book. This is how like the original Bible was never translated because nobody knows how to speak the language that it is in.

They revise the Bible, add things, change things. So they keep you in the dark. By not letting you know how great of a people that you were, and how strong, and how you survived. If we don't know that, then we definitely don't care what happens today.

There is an interesting hidden assumption behind all this talk about the teacher conspiracy. Only school teachers can supply the truth—not parents, not peers, not experience. Egleston kids believe that school is their only possible savior, and yet they feel utterly betrayed by school. Public schools are part of the great conspiracy to cleanse the imperial past, to portray the savagery of Americans as benign neglect. The kids believe parents have failed to nourish them intellectually, and the ghetto culture has left them untutored and ignorant. Most ignore the church. They know the community has disintegrated and the commitment to learn is absent. They are in the extraordinary situation of needing a link to the outer world, but they believe white teachers have betrayed them. They don't know it, but they want elders, learned in the lore and glory of black and Latino history. Everything else is mundane or a lie. This, among other things, is how extreme social disorganization destroys lives.

People are what they know. That's who you are, all you've learned. Well, we've learned shit, and it's not all our fault. The schools, white teachers, you know, Irish and Italian, they hate us. Don't teach us. Don't help us. It is planned. It is planned. It is on purpose to keep us stupid and weak.

We know where things are going. We know what the cops have in mind. They would like to destroy us and so would Washington, then they don't got this problem in mind, no ghetto, no crime, no drugs. They getting nowhere now. Things the same, year after year—gang wars, poverty, welfare, no jobs, lousy schools. Boston is O.K. downtown, and we got shit. Know what I mean?

They don't want to help. They can't fix it up, too expensive. So they don't tell us the truth about our history. They purposely teach us wrong, and it's all in preparation to get rid of us. It's the best solution for them. They don't even have to kill us because we so out of it we may as well be gone. This whole thing is about life and death. And you don't need to die to be dead. Look at the kids who can't read ten pages, can't stop tapping their feet, can't pay attention. They are really dead.

The president is the cause of these crimes. He and the IRS mastermind the plot against minorities, which is executed by Congress, mayors, and the police. Not educating minorities is the first part of a preparation plan to destroy black and Hispanic culture. Congress, for example, oversees schools of education and approves the books and curriculum that distorts black history.

Teachers are carefully trained to provide minority kids with inferior pedagogy. This is the liturgy. The black and Latino curriculum is purposely simplified and purged:

Here's the biggest lie they tell you. Children in the inner city are dropping out due to their friends or drugs. That ain't why niggers is dropping out nowadays. Because you all don't give us the type of education we need, don't tell us what our race has been through. You can't know where you're going if you don't know where you came from.

Well, if we lie to them about their history, that's all we have to do. We can learn the math and stuff like that, but fuck it. If we don't know history, then we don't really know nothing because we're not going nowhere because we're not seeing anything and we're not being focused on anything.

School committees deliberately refuse to repair ghetto schools and replace books. The lines are drawn:

They got the guns and the school and the teachers. But we got the brothers. And the hood teaches us how to survive and hide and join, and it won't be so easy to beat us in a guerilla war. Someday the black and Hispanic and Asian and all the others got a majority. Then you wait. The Bible says we're going to inherit the Earth. you know, the meek—well, that's us. Not today. Maybe in a few years another "big bang."

Egleston is rich in black and Latino history and literature, and the teachers and social workers are caring and patient. The atmosphere is nourishing. Everyone can get individual help. For many Egleston kids, the school is a second home. But, as I've said, on any given day half the student body is absent. Many students cannot pay attention for more than a few minutes, and very few become committed to a particular subject. There are exceptions, but not many. The students have been mishandled for so many years that some peculiar disintegration has muted their effect and fractured their interest in the world beyond Egleston Square. The issue for many students is survival. School is a peripheral activity.

The pathetic education these students have had in their previous high school (almost all are dropouts), amounts to an intellectual malnutrition that permits their fantasies to remain unchecked by reality. They live in a rich imaginative world full of demons and dragons poised to devour them.

Many Egleston students, usually the less sophisticated, have concocted a Wagnerian scenario of triumph and redemption that compensates for their powerlessness:

You know the writing is on the wall. By fifty or sixty years from now, most of the people in America will not be white. Maybe seventy to eighty years. When that day comes, blacks, Hispanics, Asians, and other minorities unite, and we got two ways to go. We elect. We fight. No one can stop us. We learned from them. Our troubles have made us tough.

The fantasy life of the kids is invariably apocalyptic—an infinitely powerful guerrilla army confronts and destroys the leviathan. No complex structural forces or subtle gradations of power obfuscate this dualism. It is we and they, good and evil, victim and victimizer. Egleston students do not act. They are acted upon. The enormous power they attribute to authority allows them to play the role of powerless victim.

It also relieves them of responsibility for their lives. The violence and the failure of the police to solve many homicides have created an atmosphere that convinces some Egleston kids that the authorities want a large-scale gang war that will eliminate the dealers, the thieves, the murderers, and the black population—a state induced genocide. Some of Egleston's more manic kids believe a holocaust is possible. They remind each other that when slavery ended, racism became the final American solution:

Why not? The Germans did it to the Jews. Look at Africa. World is full of hatred and jealousy, and the holocaust makes a lot of money and gets everybody excited and unite with leaders who give permission to kill. They would do this to us if they could get away with it. They have done everything else. Why not this? These whites are not human. White people trained to hate us.

The more sophisticated students, Robert and Felicia, for example, assume that black and Latino history is a seamless web: the murderous past shapes the racism of the present. Robert, perhaps the brightest boy at Egleston, said, "History is something you can't get out of, can't escape. The past and the present are one and the same. The future grows from the past. You know what I mean. Our chances are not good. The past makes us."

Despite the gloom, Robert and a few Egleston kids continue to believe that adversity strengthens the soul. "Brutality," Felicia remarked, "will toughen us." Robert agreed:

We the way we are because slavery and racism. They took us from Africa in chains, and then they freed us, that's a joke. And then for a hundred, a hundred and thirty years, fucked us. We are not dumber than they are. We are better than they are. There is something pure about us. Despite the dope.

Pure. They have made us by their hatred. Their hatred brought us brothers
together and taught us how to survive.

Nobody but black people call each other brother. We got a community.
And we get a few skills and education, we are not going to fuck each other
like white men do. It's money and selfishness. Everybody fuck everybody
else for the money. Whites teach us who the enemy is. And whites teach
us how to beat other people. We follow them, and we rule. Everything
reverses in life. We are learning. They force us to learn, to survive. We do
jobs, and we learn.

Felicia understood the inversion Robert preached, the inversion of
master and slave during which the slave becomes proficient in work and
life, rich in ego and spirit, while the master becomes indolent, superfluous, and impotent. This insight is at the heart of apocalyptic politics and
Marxism. The proletariat suffers, becomes class conscious, liberates itself
and mankind, and creates a non-alienated world. These kids know
nothing about Marxism or radicalism, but they understand in some
arcane way that oppression can stimulate opposition and exploitation
can unite the exploited: "Their crime and crazy sex made them wicked
and hateful while we be pure and moral. We have brothers. They got
people who hate and fuck each other."

Despite their faith in the apocalypse and the transformation of evil
into good, slave into master, Felicia does not believe that a dramatic
increase in the black and Latino population will cause a corresponding
shift in power:

White men will never surrender. They will find ways to protect their money
and business, and they will know how to keep us closed in. Look at Los
Angeles. Black people destroy black property, not white's. Even when blacks
and Hispanics got the majority, more of us than them, you know what I
mean, we still lose. They got the money, and they know how to lie to folks.

That's the job of candidates. Look at Roxbury and Dorchester, same shit, same poverty.

David, the third member of the trio, listens to Felicia as if she were his alter ego. He mouths words when she talks and shakes his head in approval. David makes loud noises that sound like words, but there is little sense behind the sounds. Many kids at Egleston rarely talk. They are part of a large silent majority—mute, stolid, shut up inside, so angry or so disconnected they can barely utter a coherent phrase. The silent majority of these students seem as if it were waiting for some cue comforting enough to reveal who they are and what they think. The kids at Egleston, and I suspect black and Latino kids in most ghettos, are verbal time bombs, armed with hundreds of ideas on all kinds of subjects, some ridiculous, others poetic and profound. Their silence is a sign of suffering or fear. Their talk, a cascade of words and screaming that comes from some cavernous inner world of repressed secrets and sorrows, responds at times to a simple human touch, a little interest, or the assurance that words will not be met with disrespect.

After months at Egleston, during which I revealed some of my own sorrow and fear—months when I asked for little and assured the kids that my respect for them would be earned by their simple honesty, months of waiting and listening—the kids at Egleston began to talk and talk about the most intimate details of their lives:

Yeah, sure I did all those things. I sold crack and cocaine, night after night, freezing, three or four in the morning waiting for some crazy customer who could shoot me for ten bucks. And the police come and steal the stuff, and you got nothing but a slap across the face. And I stole, broke into houses and stole from people on the street. And for a while, I was a prostitute, but I didn't like it. Meanwhile my boyfriend gets the money, and I get slapped around. I live with another girl now. My mother's out of it, father's gone.

How you expect me to go to school and study? You tell me. With a life like mine, the problem is to stay alive, not go to school. Murray, many of my friends are dead.

One teacher told me, "These kids have no ideas, and they have no politics." She was wrong. Egleston and probably thousands of high schools are full of kids who have thought about white power and their own powerlessness, kids who think about liberation and servitude. The kids at Egleston are full of politics. They think about the meaninglessness of elections and the myths and symbols used to stabilize society. Their hatred of the state and politicians is deep. Many of their ideas are absurd and fantastic, but they have a political philosophy, parts of which are subtle and sophisticated. And they are not reluctant to discuss their hate and hope, their thoughts about their powerlessness and what liberation might mean. In fact, their political ideas make those of most suburban kids look painfully patriotic and unaware.

David, who spoke only occasionally during our long conversation, produced a theory laced with fact and fantasy that exemplified the first principles of Egleston politics: The white man's gain must result in the minorities' loss, and the real issue is class conflict:

And we know what is wrong. We know what our people need and don't know. Obviously, when you put us into power, we're going to help our own, right? They're going to have to get rid of us, the people who don't like what we're doing. They call the CIA.

It is not hard to figure out. There is you and us, and we at ends with each other. Ask who owns this country and who owns the ghetto. It ain't us. No, it ain't us. We are owned, we're not owners. Business is not fun for us. It's for profit, so they not going to let us have stores, businesses. Because what we got they don't. Not a question of love or hate. A question of profit and loss.

The more we lose the more they make. They keep telling us you can make it, but you don't believe it. It's bullshit propaganda.

David had introduced the theme that dominates the thinking of many bright Egleston students: white men will have to eliminate blacks and Latinos when they become a serious threat. The management of ghetto people will be planned in secret and executed by the CIA and the Secret Service. Minorities are so dangerous and cunning that only master intelligence operatives could control them. This perception reflects the megalomania of the students, but it also reflects their powerlessness. The idea of class conflict and exploitation is alien to most Americans, but it is familiar to some Egleston kids who think of America as a zero sum game. They are aware of the gap between political rhetoric and reality, one of several reasons why they have no faith in the future. They are the other America, and they know it. The kids believe that there will be a black holocaust but also that black and Latino power will ultimately triumph. Egleston students frequently advance incompatible ideas because they are badly educated and know very little about the world beyond the ghetto. They need to invent optimistic outcomes to compensate for reality. There is relief and pleasure in smashing reality, even if it is through fantasy. The esprit de corps of Egleston students is forged in part by perceiving white men as depraved, obscene, devious, and sexually aberrant in contrast to their community of brothers, where mutual aid takes precedence over money making. The dehumanizing of whites is a common theme; their depravity is a benchmark by which minorities measure their purity.

They fuck all the time, anybody, anywhere. They don't care who it is. They are always getting divorced, and it is usually because they found a better fuck. And they are led by their prick, their penis, and it's not even that they fuck. They like oral sex, you know, sucking dicks. That's why they get so much AIDS. But it's not just sex that's so weird. It's stealing, by not stealing. Doing white business means fucking competitors and customers and paying the government to get favors. Because they fuck like wildfire anyway. And they don't really care too much for condoms and that stuff because they get on. The systematic sex stuff, like sucking dicks and oral sex, all that crazy stuff. Know what I'm saying? But here in our communities, we have sex, we feel like brothers. I've gotta throw a "Jimmy" on.

So there are two conflicting views of the future. In the first, minorities triumph through purity of heart and numbers in a peaceful electoral transfer of power. In the second scenario, America decimates blacks and Latinos, relegating them to a permanent ghetto life. There is a third depressing scenario, more mundane than the others but also more realistic:

What do we do when we finish here? Slap hamburgers at McDonald's or Burger King? Clean up shit at hospitals? Drive buses? Janitor? Handyman? Dealer? They gotta get this shit done. Who going to do it? We're at the bottom of the pyramid so we do this. And for them to stay at the top, we got to stay at the bottom. They got it together. They are united, got the army and the judge, ain't neutral—they belong to them, not us. Everybody know black man go to jail longer than white men for the same crime. Ain't no justice for us, and ain't no equality. They tell you in school that everything's pretty good and people elect the government and other lies. That's why kids don't go to school, don't want a lot of bullshit. It's too bad. Shit, man, teach me. Teach me!

Robert supports this bleak but largely accurate forecast by insisting that America is an oligarchy—the state is the instrument of the ruling class, if you will. The great corporations ultimately control America, so the hope of a black-Latino takeover in the mid-twenty-first century is unrealistic. Where there is no economic power there can be no political power:

Economic power, not numbers, determines what occurs in political history. Money pays the bills for elections, and money determines what happens to government. The big corporations may not get everything. They won't, but they can stop what they don't want. This is why we have cigarettes, and they kill people. So don't think when the time comes and we outnumber seventy to eighty million or more that we are going to win. No, we're still going to lose because we don't control businesses. Government is for sale, and the currency is not votes. Money buys influence. Money buys respect, and money buys education. Without money, how are we going to get to college? We don't see anyone but blacks and Hispanics. We are students and people who don't know anything. Dumb makes dumb. This is where they want us, enclosed and dumb. We can't get unified. All this talk about black and Hispanic take over. Bullshit! Don't even talk good English. How can we pass the college exam?

Felicia and Robert talked a lot about how poorly the kids at Egleston speak:

Nobody is going to hire us. We can't even speak English good. We speak black English and Spanish, and anyone can tell that, and then they know we are uneducated. So good language is part of getting out of here. But this is not so bad because so many whites are dumb and can't speak either.

Robert believes that the rich prevail in Congress, and he is convinced that blacks and Latinos will not become a serious force until they accumulate capital. There is no doubt in his mind that the state spends substantial effort camouflaging the class system with egalitarian myths and pacifying minorities by miseducating them:

They don't really tell us about how the system is. The system is made of a pyramid. Us so-called minorities are at the bottom. The low class ain't getting nowhere; won't let us build. Then you have the middle class, but then you have the top of the pyramid—that's where the president and all the rich people are. So they're the ones who are making the pyramid for us—let's keep them at the base. You know what I'm saying? There's three levels, and you have to start at the bottom. They are already on top.

They don't teach us about that shit in Boston schools. They don't want us to think we are on the bottom and because they keep us there, they teach everybody in America is equal. That equal shit is to fool us, make us believe we got a chance when we don't. They figure the less we know about the pyramid the more we believe it's a normal thing—you know, not created by them.

If we do better, they do worse, so they have to keep us poor. They need us poor to do all the crap they don't want to do. Nothing changes. It can't. They don't want it to change because change means they worse off. They can't let us get skills. We take their jobs. Not going to happen.

David, absolutely silent for several minutes and apparently bored by all this talk about class and pacification, suddenly awoke from his private world and referred to Robert and Felicia's earlier comments about the power of language:

Robert's saying we are killing our language, destroying our ability to talk. If you can't talk or be understood, you are fucking dead, alone, lost. Can't get a job. Who the fuck is going to hire my friends, the way they talk? Robert is right. We get worse because we talk to each other and no one else so the mistakes, the mistakes get more and larger. And it's all because we live in the same area, all black, all Hispanic, a few others, so don't you think whoever keeps us together and prevents people of different, what's the word, different ethnics from mixing. And who is it that locates all of us, and I mean all of us, in one big, Felicia calls it a big brown bag that they shake with us inside. It's poverty that does this and no jobs and it's racism. It's the only place we can afford.

The laws of life and language have produced a language functional for the ghetto, an arcane English, as the ghetto moves away from white America. Language is the measure of apartheid. Robert spoke of education as power. David now described language as power.

David's insights reveal a kind of thoughtful and agitated mental motion that quivers below what looks like a vacuous surface. When I came to know fifteen or twenty Egleston kids, I realized there were two worlds—each kid was two kids, two lives, two minds. Everyone was both himself or herself and another person locked in a prison of fear or rage. The interior discourse was hidden by bravado or withdrawal or depression or mania or imitative autism. The key that unlocked the inner chamber was not surrendered quickly. First came school, then trust, then a few guarded questions about parents that often touched the kids' hatred of absent fathers and their feelings for mothers too desperate and hard-working to be reached.

I interviewed sixty-three Egleston students, some for hours. During three years and hundreds of hours of talk, I found that almost without exception during the first interview my questions were answered with obvious, simple, uninformative, straightforward answers: "My father works in some market." "My mother works in a hospital. That's all." The real pain was reserved for later talks when the kids at Egleston lowered their masks and revealed the malignant fabric of their lives.

You talk about learning and having a chance. There is no chance. Two brothers in jail for selling drugs. Father gone. I have no skills, not a mechanic or carpenter or anything else. The school taught me about reading and some math and the teacher taught about Hispanic history. How is that going to help me? That's why I feel like shit. Can't get of bed. Nothing to get out for.

That's why I come to school late or I be absent. I can't see how my life is going to change; that's what gets me so low. No future, no jobs, no change. Tell me, Murray, what can I do? What is my skill? Nothing.

Segregation insulates these kids. They may be twenty chronologically, but emotionally many are actually ten or twelve. Many live in high-rise public housing, brick boxes with rows of windows, lined up like lifeless soldiers, paramilitary enclaves. And they spend most of their lives within a few blocks of the project. For these kids, Boston is a distant land, easily accessible by subway but a place where parochial survival skills won't work. There is much swaggering, but the fact is these kids are afraid of failing in a white world. They feel uncomfortable away from the hood, foreshortened, and anxious. Egleston Square reminds me in many ways of a medieval *shtetl*, a self-enclosed Jewish village where religious ortho-doxy bred true believers, fearful for the future and the outside world, separated physically and ideologically from Christians. Jews became increasingly inbred. The *shtetl* and the ghetto are solitary confinements in which what is will become more so.

The kids' insecurity became clear when I arranged internships for two boys, one of whom wanted to become a sound engineer, the other an architect. A Boston television station was happy to train our engineer, and a well-known architect agreed to take an intern. These were unusual opportunities. But neither boy could phone their mentor or visit his office. They lied to me every week: "The phone is out of order," "the phone is busy," "Mr.——— is out of town," etcetera. The project died. These boys were afraid they would fail. But *I* actually failed them. I should have driven them, but I was caught up in the stupid, and in this case, inappropriate ideal that these kids must learn to be self-reliant, adult, and tough. In fact, they had been so injured that they needed a helping hand. A personal introduction to the architect and the station manager would have assuaged much anxiety. These boys and girls, I knew well, accepted the racial and ethnic boundaries that insinuate themselves into the conscious and unconscious mind and are then transformed into custom. The eternal dichotomy of we and they, black and white, rich and poor, is constantly reaffirmed by reality. It is this isolation and separation, this pathological inbreededness, this kind of social "incest" that traumatizes and truncates these kids.

The kids at Egleston are not bound to their turf by religious orthodoxy or state policy, although the police may harass them and demand to know where they live. They live within four or five square miles. They commune with the same kids and neighbors; they belong to the same gangs; they know the same merchants; they are lured by the same enticements. But, unlike middle-class kids, they talk to each other, their peers in class, and literally no one else. Their language becomes increasingly archaic and less acceptable to American commerce. Egleston Square, year by year, becomes increasingly separated and alienated from middle-class America. The kids at Egleston know this reality, one reason why they believe their life chances are poor. I emphasize once again that these kids feel they have been deliberately robbed of a glorious past of military heroes, builders, poets, and painters. With no past, they feel formless, without identity. Since they are without ancestors, without training and without jobs, they also see no future. The present is therefore all they have. There is no reason to wait, no reason to look back. The violence of the ghetto, the erosion of values, and the generally indifferent attitude to school and life are enhanced by this obliteration of time. Like the Americans described by Tocqueville, Egleston kids are preoccupied with the present and immediate gratification:

You are surprised we are not interested in tomorrow. Why should we be interested in tomorrow? What's tomorrow got for us that we don't have now? Jobs? Money? College? Respect?

You know and so do we, only skilled jobs, and we don't got the skills. So why should we think future? Our problem is now, today, thinking about how to get home safe. Think about it, how to get home safe from school.

Felicia was one of a small group of students who remained optimistic despite the deterioration around her. She was convinced that whites would have to train blacks and Latinos because they need skilled labor, and this training would transform power relations:

We are going to be where they are. They can't stop us because as employees they must teach us their skills. And when we learn their skills, we will replace them because we quicker and tougher. And the more skills we have got, the more jobs we qualify for. I don't think it is school that will get us through. It will be training jobs. Of course, this a reason they won't train us. We are going to get stronger while they get rich and fat. Some day we will become them and they will become us. Not just the change in black and Hispanic numbers. It's the change in what we learn and can do.

Like Felicia, Robert saw liberation through education but felt that schools were part of the political apparatus and therefore devoted to maintaining a black and Latino underclass. Schools would really educate minorities only when they were separated from political control, something Robert did not believe would happen:

It's bullshit. We all know that politicians are bullshit. White folks may be dumb enough to believe it, but we know politics like dope. It quiets people down, you know, the "Star Spangled Banner" and Fourth of July shit. You can get the truth. They don't want you to have it because they use the lies to control us. They use them in the schools, and they use them in politics. Powerful people have to lie because they don't want others to see how they got power and how they use it. They are crooks. They get there by raising millions, and they pay back the companies that gave them money.

So they lie and talk about government by the people. So what do you think if politicians lie all the time, what about teachers and ministers? They are part of the power, so they got to lie, too. So how we going to find what's real? How we going to find out who we are, who is fucking us where we come from? If we can't know what's real—the facts—we are lost, hopeless. If we're lost, how are we going to find ourselves? We have to teach ourselves, or we have to use our emotions to get out of this. They don't want us to know.

In a moment that may prove prophetic, Robert, like rebels before him, has concluded that minorities will have to educate themselves and not merely because the schools are biased. The entire society is wedded to existing arrangements, pacified by the state and the media, and not seriously committed to ending racism.

The kids at Egleston shuttle between acute observation and nonsense because they know so little. Robert, the most sophisticated boy I knew at Egleston, the only student who read newspapers and frequently watched the news on television, exemplified this split, this flight to fancy and return to reality. If politicians are bullshit, liars and crooks, I asked Robert, how did the American government function?

The American government is like a drug corporation. The IRS is at the head. Then comes Congress, the Senate, the president, and the CIA. The IRS is like the Colombians. The Congress is the Mafia. The Senate is the hit men. And the president's the drug dealer. But then y'all say, "how is that possible?" The IRS gets the taxes and the money and stuff like that, that pays the Congress, the Senate, and the president, and stuff like that. The Congress can't get paid until they go see the IRS, and the IRS has to feel that they are doing right by them. The IRS gotta feel like, "I don't like that law you're passing by decreasing the taxes on certain people. If you're going to do that, then I gonna just cut you." The president is just there to fuck everybody plain up, but he doesn't because he is getting paid enough. See, the president knows everything cause they have to tell the president everything. He's getting his money; he's not saying nothing. The money in the government flows around the government—it don't flow nowhere else. The government runs the money. We have no say so. We bust our ass. We're making $6.50 an hour—in reality we're making about five, maybe four something. In order to keep paying the people at the top, they have to keep taxing, because the people at the top get more greedier.

They started making things like the DEA, FBI, the CIA. Know what I'm saying? Secret Service. All they do is kill secretly. Who are they killing? Anybody that opposes them. Any examples? Noriega. The cartel family. The DEA, the CIA brought them down. Why? Because the cartels weren't kicking them on no more loot. The cartels were billionaires. They own Florida. Doesn't the government do a lot of business with the cartel? That's the main reason why they had to bring them down—because the cartels didn't want to do no more business with them. The cartels was like, "Man, fuck them, we can make our own money. They can't fucking handle us. We running Florida. They need us for their shit. We're the ones keeping the government controlled"—and stuff like that. Then they send the DEA and the CIA to put the hit on them. That's why they're so secretive.

Robert's discourse is staccato. He has no doubts. The facts are obvious to him. Secrets and mysteries that have troubled social scientists for years are revealed to Robert because he assumes the government and the ghetto operate in the same way. The ghetto is his model, a miniversion of the United States. The ghetto is basically a giant drug operation, the only enterprise that generates enough profit to dominate the local economy and law enforcement. The power of money is magnified by the absence of other resources. The U.S. government, Robert argues, is actually headed by the IRS, a conspiratorial agency that controls the distribution of funds and public policy. The president is paid off, just like the cops and local politicians. The government, like everything in the ghetto, is about money. Everyone and every institution can be bought off, every cop, every politician. The state, like dealers and real estate owners, circulates money among its own but never permits the flow to go beyond political boundaries. Like most alienated voters, Robert assumes that politicians are corrupt and that it makes little difference who wins elections. Politicians are a cash crop, owned by investors. Robert's interpretation of American politics is gradually becoming an American view.

Lawlessness and conspiracy are the essential attributes of the state. The DEA and FBI and CIA kill everyone that opposes them. They do it secretly, and they do it for money. This is the underlife of the ghetto magnified to national and international dimensions. The war of all against all is the only life Robert knows. Yet he also sees beyond the typical alienated voter. For him, American society, as well as politics, is mystified by political rhetoric:

They love that shit, the "Star-Spangled Banner," and the Fourth of July, the fireworks in the Charles River, and all that terrible shit about brotherhood. I suppose each country has its ways of keeping folks together. Isn't the election to tell people everything O.K.? The people will vote in the politics. And they will be on top. White folks eat up this shit. But we know it's shit.

But things different at Egleston Square. We get some real history. We get black history and Hispanic history, real history, only here we get a chance to find roots. White people laugh when we talk about roots, but they know who they are, long back. We know we got a great history in Africa and South America, great civilizations. But that's not what teachers tell in Boston. It's Paul Revere and George Washington. What do they have to do with us? Nothing! American history teachers teach to respect the flag and the Constitution and know what the Fourth of July stands for.

This is just another way of saying we should respect America and shut the fuck up.

Although a few kids see through some American myths, they have no idea that their views are self-justifying. The kids I interviewed talk with certainty. The students are sure they know how things work. This sureness makes them haughty, but it also makes them feel weak because they see America as an imperial, aggressive empire beyond their control. They do not entertain the notion that political consciousness might be a precondition for liberation. They rarely talk about how they might escape from the ghetto. Felicia insisted that even Robert failed to appreciate how little freedom blacks and Latinos have in comparison to whites. For her, America was a tundra where ghetto kids were frozen in place.

I know that much of my life was set before I was born. It was set by the fact that I'm Hispanic. It was set by the racism of the white men who put us in the brown-bag ghetto, and they decide what we can and cannot expect. Sure, they let a few of us out to succeed and then show us as examples of how good America is. You know, Michael Jordan. But, man, they have all the power and we in the bag don't even know who we are. We are always being manipulated and we don't even know it because it's all we know. We don't have a history; here we don't change; we're not in control.

Egleston students turn away from themselves to the external world for explanations, where more tangible enemies can be identified—racist teachers, crooked cops, corrupt politicians. Their search for external enemies does not imply that their theories are wrong or crazy. It simply means that they are fixated on historians as liars and history as subjugation. Felicia was always quick to remind us, "History, you know it is *his* story, not *our* story. It is to keep us down. There is no accurate record of the past. They rewrote the record. History is their make-believe."

History may be fiction, but the students do not see themselves as makers of their own history. They are powerless and passive victims of global cabals. These ways of looking at the world encourage all kinds of unrestrained behavior. Contempt for white society, government, and the legal system—in addition to contempt for history—makes the students moral free agents. The judicial system is corrupt and guilt and innocence are hypocritical judgments. Therefore, criminal activity, as it were, doesn't exist.

Felicia was caught selling marijuana on school grounds, and her boyfriend was convicted for carrying unlicensed firearms. These experiences confirmed her view that the criminal justice system was corrupt:

I'll give you an example how the government works. O.K.? I went to visit my boyfriend one day in jail, all right? He caught with a gun, right? That's one year mandatory. They tried to give him six to ten years. O.K.? He's been in there three years. He got caught on one charge, and they tried to bring up all the other ones. When I went to visit him, he pointed out a white man to me. He killed four people. In a car accident. He was under the influence of everything. You know what he got off with? Two years, the most for killing four people. Now you tell me. What's that? Murdering four people or carrying a bullshit gun—that's one year. And they give them six to ten years—because he had his family, is in the state house. He got off with that. The idea of equal justice ain't true. That's bullshit. There is no equal justice.

Robert described the disparity between black and white justice in more graphic terms:

These textbooks tell you like, they set up the Bill of Rights, here for everybody. Know what I'm saying? In the Constitution, everybody is supposed to be treated in the same ways, sort of, and stuff like that. We're not treated in the same fashion. Know what I'm saying? We live in the inner city, we get beat up by cops, we get shot at. We kill somebody, we get life. If the cops kill somebody, they get off with pay and a vacation. *We* got mother fuckers in the suburbs killing their whole god damned families and they get off in two years. Know what I'm saying? Because, oh, they say they was crazy, so why don't I go to court, kill somebody, and say I was crazy and get under two years? They don't even go to the same jails we do. They go to the fucking state farms and stuff like that. You know what I'm saying? That's kiddie shit. They could just go there, tell the court they're crazy, the court's sitting there. They wait about a couple of months and "I'm sane now, guys, let me go." And they'll let them go. Know what I'm saying? The system, you know, ain't set up for us.

To these kids, the moral depravity of the government and white America is beyond doubt. The ultimate proof cited by blacks throughout the country is a series of medical experiments performed by white government doctors on black patients between 1932 and 1972 in which 399 black men with syphilis were denied treatment. The Tuskegee experiment, as it was called, provides many blacks with verification of white perfidy and lends credence to the idea of a black holocaust. The story of these experiments frequently appears in black publications. Robert had read the story several times.

They created AIDS since the Vietnam War. The government and their scientists and labs and whatever. AIDS, O.K., when they went to Vietnam War, they shot them up with something, and they said to soldiers it would not show up until ten years late. AIDS doesn't show up until ten years later. The scientists have their own place. They test diseases every day just as they did down south with all the young black men. They said, "Oh, we're going to test you" or . . . like TB, I forgot what it was. Instead they shot them up with syphilis or with gonorrhea. They shot them up with a disease that sterilizes you, and they only did this to black men. They say, "Oh, keep coming back," and that's when they started testing the penicillin. They . . . "Oh, let's see if this cures them." They were using us as their guinea pigs so they can further themselves.

In 1990, the School of Public Health at the University of North Carolina, Chapel Hill, informally surveyed about one thousand black church members in five cities, a large but not statistically representative sample. One-third of the respondents believed "the AIDS virus was produced in a germ warfare laboratory as a form of genocide against blacks." Almost one-third of the respondents in every study believe there is some truth to the report that the AIDS virus was produced in a germ warfare laboratory to eliminate black people.

Many blacks, like Robert, believe genocide by AIDS is a perfectly rational policy given the history of slavery and the abuse of black America. I asked Robert if the virus was created to kill blacks, why do so many whites get AIDS?

They have a cure because they made it. If you pay enough, sure, they will give it to you. See, they brought the drugs into the black, Latino, and Puerto Rican communities, and we were selling the drugs. But you don't make that much money selling drugs in your community, because statistics show that not many blacks, and Latinos, and Puerto Ricans smoke crack. More white people do it. They brought their drugs to Wall Street, so now it's an epidemic. Say a black or a Latin or somebody caught AIDS or something. He went and had sex with a white person, and now the disease is spreading around there like wildfire because they fuck like wildfire anyway.

These are doctors who are supposed to cure disease, not cripple people, government doctors who lie to blacks and sterilize blacks and then they keep it a secret. Doesn't impress white people. I don't see it in history textbooks. If you really hate someone, niggers, you can do anything to them, and it don't look weird to you. It's all part of a day's work, like lynching.

The profoundly immoral nature of these white government doctors was revealed to Robert by the fact that they not only lied about the experiment but also selected only black men, treated them as subhuman, and kept their work secret. The most hideous aspect of the experiment for Robert was the fact that many subjects became sterile. Robert saw the doctors who were supposed to cure people as subhuman and an example of the enormous gulf that separates the races. According to Robert, the experiment was not weird to white doctors; it was all part of a day's work.

The mundane quality of white atrocities kept Felicia, Robert, and David talking about white elections and white justice:

Elections is for them. For whites, not us. They be dumb enough to believe they important—they make no difference, you know what I mean. Same people govern, rich people, influential people. But they got to get the big numbers, the American people, not to see what goes on so they got these bullshit ideas about government by the people, and people has rights. So they get people to believe and they be quiet and they vote. These bullshit ideas keeps white people in line. But we are not that dumb. We know elections are bullshit. There is white justice and black justice and white rights and black. Know what I'm saying? And they got to not only get them to be quiet and vote and accept. You know what I mean. They got to train them to buy and buy, get to the malls and buy stuff, because that's what keeps the economy going. Got to have a good economy to get the taxes for the government. So it's a big selling job.

The trio believes that white people are dupes, citizens who by habit or some irrational reason vote regularly but do not understand political reality. Democracy is an enormously successful ideology, but America is for the few. Whites need "democratic" ideas to convince them that politics is important and the people govern: "The bullshit idea keeps

people in line." Felicia and Robert are impressed by the irrationality of
politics and the ability of men of power to pacify through words and
symbols. The United States is governed in fact by "rich people, influential people," but the American people do "not see what goes on."

Robert and Felicia, however, also understand that consumption and
pleasure are intimately connected to political stability and, therefore, to
pacification. The state and the culture must train people "to buy and
buy, get to the malls and buy stuff. So it's a big selling job." In a crude
and simplistic way, these students touch upon Herbert Marcuse's idea
of pacification through pleasure—the argument that affluence, high
levels of consumption, and the pleasures they bring have become the
mechanism for pacifying people in advanced countries:

You cannot be happy in America unless you can make enough money to
buy all the things TV tells you need. And this country has a long list of what
you need to be happy and a real American. So they have to have prosperity
to pull this off. So this is one reason why the kids are not smiling. They
can't afford to, but when they get some money, what do they do? Buy leather
jackets or fancy clothes. This is what makes them happy. It's what makes
Americans happy.

The implications of Robert's ideas, though he doesn't extend them,
are Orwellian: the control of political language is the ultimate power.
Language is the ultimate seductress. Language defines reality. Language
may depict reality for whites, but Robert and a small number of Egleston
students insist that the hard facts of life, the cold reality of the ghetto,
is too solid to be manipulated by language or myth. The facts of life are
to etched in stone: the poverty, the crime, the unemployment: "But we
are not that dumb. We know elections are bullshit."

A few of the more sophisticated students predicted that the state's
efforts to pacify blacks and Latinos through myth and ritual would fail

because they are aliens in America and thus immune. In theory, this ability to separate illusion and reality in politics will be an immense asset when minorities do become the majority. "We will wait," David said, reiterating a common Egleston theme, "and we will see. We know their shit now. We are on to them. They can't bullshit us anymore."

Since Robert was talking about pacification and power, I asked why politicians run for office.

Because then they could feel the power. That they have power. It can make all their dreams come true. And if you are not rich, you have no power. Know what I'm saying? If you could run for a government office and win, you get power and respect. They want control. Control over everybody and everything. To make their dreams come true. Government serves the people with money that pay them. People who are putting money in their pocket. We are. Companies, businesses, that's why they protect those companies and industries.

This is a description of gang life in Egleston Square. The gang seeks power and money. Status is critical. Respect is critical. Control is critical. The gangs in Boston's ghetto seek more turf and total control. The gang, like the state, rewards its friends and punishes its enemies. But the ultimate issue is always power. The pragmatic and unprincipled politics of America and the crescendo of cash required to fuel the system require the Machiavellian ethic described by Robert. Much of his thinking about politics is obviously modeled after gang life, which might provide a fruitful perspective for social scientists.

Robert was like an intellectual whirling dervish, gesticulating, yelling, always moving around the room spitting words, throwing words as if he could knock you over with them, never hesitating for a second, never looking for a phrase, talking as if he abandoned his text for a more explosive and heartfelt exposition. I knew Robert was extraordinary, but

I had no idea he was to become a close friend. He once described his dysfunctional family: a father who could not earn a living and disappeared, brothers in jail who lived by selling dope and scamming credit cards, the uncle who taught him to drive a getaway car. He fantasized about going to Virginia Tech on a football scholarship and then becoming a physical therapist. But this dream, like so many at Egleston, was not to be.

Robert read with facility, and he had a beautiful voice that reminded me a bit of Paul Robeson's. He had the ghetto version of Parkinson's disease. He couldn't concentrate. He couldn't bring a project to completion. He couldn't sit still although his monologues often lasted several minutes. But he was very bright. The jagged surface of life in the ghetto denied Robert and many others the repose necessary to relax and think.

Attention deficit syndrome was the school's public health hazard. That and agoraphobia (in this case, fear of the white world) condemned many students to a life in the hood, where they did not have to test their skills before white human resources people who knew nothing about them. In Egleston Square, Dorchester, or Roxbury, everyone knew the parochial routines of daily life, which created the feeling of a tribal and traditional society. Kids were pressured by issues of survival to follow the rules and become what others were. Over time, the kids became more "black," more "Latino," and more isolated. This homogeneous culture subtly warned kids not to be serious about school. When someone made a bright remark in class, it was not uncommon for other students to scream, "Look at that nigger." Here "nigger" meant "white" and pretentious.

We had so many twenty-year-old boys struggling with eighth-grade math and simple social science. So many teenage mothers. It was easy to give up. I had studied American history and political theory for fifty years, and it now seemed absolutely futile. All the speculation, all the public policy, all the egalitarian ideals, all the theory amounted to nothing. None of it introduced these kids to an American life. None of it mitigated the melancholy for murdered friends or affected the underground economy that thrives on dope. America had basically written off my students.

I realized that it is possible to keep people alive and drain their life force at the same time. You can maim the spirit, destroy the history, and disembowel the identity. The kids were too depressed to study, too depressed to work. Many were simply exhausted because of the death of their friends or the need to work the night shift at minimum wages and then go to school. But the ghetto itself, the filth, the decrepitude, the dealers, the liquor stores, the overarching sense that no one is going anywhere, weakens the soul and denies the possibility of life. Egleston was not just a school for me, not just the last good deed of my life at age seventy, but a holy place, like a library or a bookstore, a sacred place where the record of life is kept. And I wanted these kids to know that record and enjoy learning about it.

One of the very best students I taught at Egleston talked about how difficult it was for her to study:

How am I going to study nights? My father in jail most of my life, dope and guns; and my mother works all day, drinks, and takes dope. No time for me. No place to study, no one tell me study is important. I got other to take care of. I feel so bad about my mom, and I get so angry I don't know what to do. Who guides me? No one. Sometimes I want to go back and be a kid with a good mother or my mother and father fixed. I feel so lonely some of the time.

I was talking to a very angry and tough Latino boy about his troubles at school—about how hard it was to pay attention and study—when he suddenly and with much bitterness began to talk about what might have been the source of his school phobia:

My fucking father disappeared when I was one. I never saw him, and if I do, I will kill the bastard. I have a two-year-old daughter. I'm not married, but I support my little girl and I visit her every week—a long trip, but I never miss. I won't do to her what that cocksucker did to me. She is going to learn how to study. I'll help her. And she is going to do something. She will have a father who cares.

Egleston actually had few classes in the formal sense, no group of kids who showed up regularly and pursued a common curriculum. We had shifting sands, a coming and going of occasional bodies who on rare occasion did some serious work until distracted by classmates answering beepers, gossiping or playing pseudo-sexuality in class.

The school came too late for most of the kids. They were too well formed for us, too imprinted by despair and con men. Robert, for example, was a bravura figure, charismatic, physically massive, and commanding, but also frightened of failing in a white world. I often talked to him about taking a course at the Harvard Extension School, but his face would become expressionless, and he would move his feet and hands nervously when I spoke. He was concerned that he could never sit down for two hours or do the reading every week. I think he was also worried about how to get to Harvard Square, how to talk, how to pay, and how to act with whites. The entire project was foreign and frightening to him, which—as we've seen—is how many of the students feel about getting a job outside the ghetto. Conversely, I am sure that potential employers would find these kids too unreliable, unskilled, and inarticulate. The chaos of Robert's family life disrupted his ability even to think. There was no stillness in Robert, no discipline. When he left Egleston, I felt an ache in my heart because in my fantasy life I was counting on him to become an agent for some not-well-defined future good, a political social worker, a teacher, an illuminator.

The world of Robert, Felicia, and David is dichotomous and conspiratorial: rich and poor, black and white, power and powerlessness,
the teachers as liars, the cops as crooks, the historian as a secret agent—
and the ultimate dualism, of course—illusion and reality. It is an inverted
world where egalitarian slogans mask inequality, schools miseducate,
and the government of the people is owned by the rich. The antinomies
clarify the confrontation and enlarge it. The victims are moralized by
their powerlessness and passivity. The malevolence of their enemies
ennobles their cause.

Egleston students are not preoccupied with time. Meals are eaten at
irregular hours, and the kids pay little attention to the time school is
supposed to begin. They often appear an hour or two late. The disappearance of time has much to do with the disappearance of jobs and of
the civic, political, cultural, and religious infrastructure that once provided an opportunity to bond. When this infrastructure collapsed, time
became even less important. There is little reason to keep time when
there is no work and little civic life. There is no reason to plan or account
for present time. The tick-tock of the modern world, the calibration that
drives the modern world, is hardly noticeable in Egleston Square. The
inability to keep track of time will significantly disadvantage these
students when and if it becomes time to work.

The discussion of time was prompted by Robert's remark, "Nothing
changes. It can't. They don't want it to change." Robert explained why
change is impossible and, by implication, why time is insignificant:

If you put me in a higher job, right, that means that you have to educate me.
That means you have to give me the tools and the knowledge to do that.

You can't give us the tools and the knowledge to run something because
if we have the tools and the knowledge, plus the money, we could become
part of your government. You can't bring nobody into the government who
is not going to support your cause. Like, you educate us, and we know what's

right, and we know what's wrong. We know what our people need and our people don't need. So, obviously, when you put us into power, we're going to help our own people, right? If you put us on the Congress, then their plan can't work. They're going to have to get rid of us. They call their boys. They call the CIA. They call the DEA. They call the Secret Service.

The federal and state government have done exactly what Robert says they will never do: create massive job retraining programs. They have made the tools and the knowledge available to many in the inner cities. His facts are wrong, but the nature of his argument is important because it is widely held. The parties are irreconcilable. Knowledge can be power if it's the right kind of knowledge. Money is power. Black profits mean white losses. The government will destroy the very people it trained if they become too powerful.

Robert describes a deadly game in which successful blacks and Latinos are liquidated. The argument is important because it is so nihilistic, an expression of such profound hopelessness and anger that its adherents— and there are probably millions—will probably surrender and remain on the fringes of the economy, on the edge of poverty, recreating the cycle of disappearing fathers, teenage mothers, and school dropouts.

I listened to variations on these themes for three years, a kind of vulgar Marxism, simplistic, pragmatic, often paranoid, often wrong, often contradictory and without historical analysis, yet in some ways instinctively solid. What accounts for this peculiar mix of intelligence, insight, and preposterous nonsense that describes the thinking of so many Egleston students? This mixture of extreme political alienation and paranoid style also characterizes right-wing militia groups. Robert and the militiamen believe a conspiracy exists to rewrite American history and to program students. He and the militiamen assume that a diabolical plot exists to magnify state power at the expense of individual rights. Both believe freedom is disappearing. Militiamen and some Egleston kids are convinced that these trends are ultimately based on the greed and lies of politicians. Both finally agree that the state has learned how to pacify the masses through propaganda and doesn't need physical force. And the republic is owned by the rich. The similarities are not exact, but the tone and mood are analogous, perhaps due to the fact that a rhetoric exists that is attractive to the plight of outsiders. Robert's argument and that of the militiamen recur periodically in American history. It recurs when some group loses status or believes the nation is falling away from first principles. The feeling of persecution is central to the argument that utilizes systematized and grandiose theories of conspiracy to explain events. The outcome, according to these views, will be apocalyptic and absolute. Richard Hofstadter refers to this reasoning as the paranoid style in American politics and argues that the style is attractive to those on the fringe of American life, those who have lost status or power, and those who wish to restore America to its golden age or to prevent change.

Robert and the militiamen live on the economical or ideological margin, and their rhetoric is the angry cry of conspiracy and loss. There are other reasons why Egleston students see the world in extremist terms, often clairvoyant, often absurd, but invariably absolute. The ghetto is a dangerous and uncertain world in which everyone tries to reduce risk and uncertainty. Many Egleston students lessen this uncertainty by conceiving the world in terms of absolutes, an obvious comfort. They see complete powerlessness and apocalyptic conspiracy, black purity and white perversion, a black holocaust and the triumph of black and Latino power. This is the local way of seeing things, perhaps an adolescent way, and an extremist way that eliminates doubt and relieves the true believer of the need to reevaluate the world.

The insight of Egleston students comes from the politics of everyday life. The dialectic of ghetto life provides them with lessons about American business and politics. They understand the importance of making and breaking alliances—gangs, if you will. And they have learned when it is wise to work cooperatively and when it is better to be a solitary entrepreneur. They have learned about wholesale and retail, price cutting and credit, gauging and monopoly, and laissez faire. They respect turf and know about private property. They have learned about the moral ambiguity of the law and the corruption of the state. The kids are profoundly alienated because they know from experience that most politicians lie and are self-serving and that many are racist. Experience has taught them that black and white justice is different and unequal. They are familiar with death and the fragile nature of the social fabric. They know that for most Americans money is what really counts. And they have learned to expect little relief.

There is a simple and straightforward way of looking at why the students mix insight with nonsense. Their lack of education forces them to extrapolate from their daily life. They have few alternative sources— an occasional TV news program, an occasional newspaper. But they know well the experiences of poverty, crime, drugs, absent fathers, hard-working parents earning little, and joblessness. They even sense that they are superfluous. This is enough experience for them to project a world external to the ghetto, an extrapolation leading to insight or nonsense depending upon whether the ghetto experience resonates with something important in American life. The exclusion of these kids occasionally leads to a plan for drastic change that exhibits both good sense and paranoia. But the fact that they produce so many bits and pieces of good sense about this country and their predicament is remarkable. Though there is much fantasy and madness, these kids are very intuitive, and living in the ghetto has taught them much about human nature and the way business and politics are conducted in America:

First, we know what's going on. Second, we are going to educate ourselves. We know what's going on so all we have to do is beat the system and become part of it. Once we educate ourselves, we can go to schools and communities and give our people that knowledge. And they will say, "So this is what's going on!" And somebody else is going to say, "Yeah, that's true. I'm stepping in." The education will give us the power to be politic. To be politic, you got to have knowledge. You got to have lying skills. If we go there knowing what we know, we dead, cause of what we know. If we go over there saying, "Well, I've read and heard that you run it like this, and like this," play dumb. *Exactly.* That's exactly how we run it. Know what I'm saying? So they thinking you don't know how it's truly run, so they keep you. "Oh, this Uncle Tom right here thinking he's helping out people. Let him do." Our brothers and sisters, we elect them to office. Then we take over.

David and Robert buttress their argument with demographics:

We are the missing 50-something percent that don't vote. If all of us vote, then they'll lose because we outnumber them three to one as a people. We did it their way, blacks, Latinos, minorities, three to four races to one.

It's not completely impossible to organize in the streets. You could do it with certain people, certain people impossible, like my cousin. If I talk to him about unity, he be like, "Fuck you, nigger. I ain't got time for that shit. I live day to day, gun to gun, sale to sale." He got kicked out of school, can't go back. The minute he lost school, it broke his hope. He's not going to be no janitor—that's degrading. If you can't go to school, how you're going to move up?

David kept shaking his head and his body as if he were in some Pentecostal church. He was a burnished version of Robert Taylor, jet-black hair combed straight back, high cheekbones, compact nose, and deeply set brown eyes that moved constantly from one person to another, like the beacon of a lighthouse. There was something aristocratic about David, as if he were excluded from the protocols of bourgeois life.

There was a disdain for daily toil, an avoidance of routine and responsibility. He gave me the feeling that he had some higher extralegal calling.
His electricity was always turned on. After his initial period of silence,
David talked constantly. Actually he screamed, as if a verbal barrage and
jagged body language would free him from the twin demons of fright
and sorrow. He was a perpetual-motion machine that produced words
at a frequency that was incomprehensible. Like Robert, David could not
sit still. He could not complete a thought. He could not listen. He had
ideas, but he could barely place them in a meaningful context. He talked
in flashes, streams of consciousness that were often indecipherable. He
was like those wild boys that periodically emerge from the wilderness,
without the order and restraint imposed by civil society. The chaos of his
conversation was the outward sign of some inner distemper. David left
school soon after I arrived, but I never forgot him.

David was preoccupied with the idea that white America intended to
keep the ghettos exactly as they were:

Those motherfuckers could stop the drugs if they wanted to, but they don't.
They got the fucking Army and Air Force and their guns. The power is
there. The desire is not. And you know why. Too much money is made by
the government from the drugs. They also get the power to stop crime.
They can do fucking anything they want. They keep us like shit, all the
ghettos, millions black and Hispanic, so they can clean the ghetto, create
jobs, stop crime. They got AIDS to kill us. Power, man, that's not the
question. It is desire.

The kids at Egleston are convinced that white America cannot
tolerate a prosperous black and Latino middle-class. The issue is not
merely that opportunities in the ghetto are few but that ghetto kids
cannot even imagine a "white" middle-class life. It is as if they were
frozen in place and time.

Felicia, whose boyfriend was in jail, believed minorities would never receive freedom in America. Mutual respect in race relations would be replaced by hatred if minorities succeed. Felicia was attractive, perhaps twenty, her large brown pupils offset by the whitest white, her skin suggesting some ancient and proud Mayan lineage. She resembled those gigantic yet beautiful and powerful women that Rivera and Orozco painted—the aquiline nose, the arched forehead, large shoulders waiting the day's work. Felicia was caring by instinct, an ombudsman for students who were depressed, grieving for friends murdered in the gang wars and the accidental shootings that pockmarked the neighborhood. She knew this silent minority, kids who move in slow motion up and down the stairs like ghosts, but she had also found life, first in a very loving mother, then in a love affair and in the school at Egleston Square, the one place where adults listened and cared.

Felicia was not afraid to tell teachers that they were boring or unclear or that they didn't understand how Latinos thought. She could deliver a rebuke, then smile. There was a diplomat in Felicia. Yet she was convinced that the white world seduced black and Latino kids to drink and take drugs. For Felicia, the neighborhood was both a jail and a madhouse, a cruel confinement that rattled the brain and the soul.

Man, I feel shaky. There's so much rattling in the hood, so much going on, gangs, dodging bullets and cops. And then I got school work. I'm sick of the hassle. The other kids need weed or drink to calm down. Surprised so much dope and liquor? I'm not. Look at all the beer the liquor store sells. The kids want peace. They want to rest. So how you rest around here?

White people are more free than we are. White people can hang out in front of their store and sit there and sell drugs and get high. No one will bother them. We can't walk down the street. If Jamaica Plain was full of white people, man, we'd be able to go hang. I can't sit in front of my house, they'll come, "Get the fuck out of here. I live here." "I don't give a fuck. Get the fuck out." Living here, this is a bigger jail. The badge gives one man too much power. "I'm gonna go and check this nigger out. You're making too much. You're making too much money. You're clockin' too much. I want a cut." That badge gives too much power.

You realize, man, what this does to people, all this hustle, "fuck you, move on," all this harassment. Everybody is nervous, unsettled, strung out. Nobody has time to think, or privacy. There's always noise. They give homework, where are you supposed to do it? No quiet. No being alone. So no homework.

CHAPTER TWO

༜

"I Don't Know What Communist Means":
The Cuban Missile Crisis

Two of my brothers in jail, for the drugs and the guns, and one of them
works. I used to sell drugs. Then, after selling drugs, that's when I started
getting into drinking and smoking herb. I used to drink every day. First it
was a weekend thing. Next thing you know it, I just said forget it, start
drinking every single day. Even used to come to school drunk. One person
in my family would die, and then once I'm gettin over that, the next person
would die. We all got a history of drinking; we all got a history of cancer.

My father died from drinking. He was in jail a lot, too. I love him, but he
used to hit my mother sometimes. I needed my father. Me and him, we just
got some kind of bond. Every time he went to jail . . . he always found his
daughter, like, "Where's my kid, where's Punkin at, I need Punkin."

Egleston teachers work in a battle zone, a neighborhood where kids
suffer from something like post-Vietnam War syndrome. Dozens of
their friends have been murdered. Dozens of fathers are absent. Egleston
students cannot be taught in traditional ways. At universities where I

lectured; my students read, wrote, and argued; and together we analyzed texts. I knew nothing about teaching high school kids, much less kids in alternative programs. It never occurred to me to ask experienced teachers how they taught. I realize in retrospect how prideful I was, the professor traveling to backward regions to spread the light.

My first course in American history was a failure and a painful beginning. For thirty-five years I had taught the freshman course in American political culture to four or five hundred students and received rave reviews, but now I could not interest ten kids at Egleston. I was furious and frustrated, actually quite depressed. I felt that the kids had launched an assault on my ego, a concerted attempt to diminish me. It wasn't true, but I was a white man and an outsider. Race was much on my mind during the first months at Egleston. My sense of being an alien sensitized me to the slightest remark. I had never met kids like this in my life, and I didn't feel comfortable. The students were not impolite, but they were cold. Most of them never responded to my hello and looked the other way when I passed. I took their silence as hostility when it was in fact shyness and discomfort. I was as strange to them as they were to me. I blamed the kids for the pitiful failure of our class. I assumed that something was wrong with them. I began to yell:

Look, you can read! You can write, damn it! You can sit on your ass and read if you want to! Did you ever think that knowledge is a weapon, yes, a weapon? More powerful than any gun you ever had. The people who changed the world didn't do it by guns, they did it by ideas. Christ, Moses, Einstein. They got an idea.

I thought Howard Zinn's *A People's History of the United States*, a history from the bottom up, would interest the kids. I was wrong:

I can't read that book. The print is too small, and the pages are too big. I don't have the time, and I don't have a quiet place at home. My mom always yellin' and my brothers are running around. Zinn's book is the same stuff over and over again—the Indians are exploited, the blacks are exploited, so are the poor. We know all this shit. Why do we need to know all these details? There was a black holocaust and still is. You don't need three hundred pages to tell us this.

How will this knowledge help us? We need stuff about how to think better. How to see what you see, the cause and the effect. We just know a few facts. We don't know why or how this works. It's all this shit about knowledge that lets them be over us. They know things that we don't. So they get the big jobs, and we got shit. We be ignorant. I ask you, how can we learn?

What do we know? How to deal. Where to buy crack cocaine, all that shit. Where to steal, what cops to pay off and avoid. We know how to steal cars and where to get guns. We in the high school of the streets, man, not where you went to school. Everything in our life stops us from thinking clear. No one read to us as kids. Everything upside down.

I did not understand when I first came to Egleston that these kids were never read to, never taken to a library, never guided to the fairy tales that enchant so many kids and whet their appetite for books. I listened for months and observed the social science class, which was chaotic and stupid. I talked to kids about life in the ghettoes of Roxbury and Jamaica Plain—how they survived; how they felt about school, their love life, their parents; what they watched on television; and how they felt about friends who were murdered. Many kids do not think about the world in linear terms. They do not frame events in terms of sequences, causes, effects, progression, regression. They view the past and today as if events occurred at random and without direction. They believe that accidents made them what they are, although some attribute their life to the ghetto. They see no long-term purpose in their history.

The connections between parents and children are severed. Events are discrete, isolated, frozen in time and out of context. Their perception is atomistic, although some kids believe in necessity:

Everybody did what they did in *Boyz n the Hood*. There are no reasons, or not many, why people do things. It's the way they are, the way they are made. You are you, and I am me, and that's what we do. I can see that some people had no choice. People are angry or sad, and that makes them. I can't remember and can't separate them. It's all like it happened yesterday— mother, father, brothers, school, the hood, all one. I can't remember when, how, I got started selling, and each day the same and nothin new. I can't see what causes me. Things happen. I don't know why.

These kids have difficulty reading, isolating critical passages, and analyzing. Their skills are more adaptive and strategic. They survive in an urban jungle. They can survive only by computing and evaluating thousands of bits of information critical for survival, bits that signify danger, truce, retreat, advance. These computations require imagination of a high order and creative intuition, the mental gymnastics of chess. The students have street smarts, an order of intelligence quite different from that of middle-class kids but equally supple. These kids are bright but distracted.

After a few months, it became clear that my students would have trouble with the classic triad, "Read this; tell me what it says; I'll tell you where you are wrong." The problem here was that the kids didn't own the material. They didn't develop it, couldn't reject it, couldn't play with it, couldn't use their imagination on it. The material was given to them, and they were instructed to repeat it. The material and their responses were static, dead, rote, and unoriginal. I made a few tentative decisions about how I would teach. My classroom material had to be like clay. The kids would sculpt and make all the creative choices. The kids would see themselves as creators. I also decided to concentrate on how to improve their thinking rather than their accumulation of knowledge. I planned to take Marx's dictum seriously. I hoped to show the class that thought is a weapon. Our subject would be dialectics, the dissection of problems, the inner movement that creates change.

I became convinced during that first year that a classical education was in order. I wanted a curriculum that stressed development, growth, cause, effect, and decay, a curriculum that stressed movement, potential, and telos, a curriculum that forced kids to think hard about where history and their lives were going. Our subject was the order and purpose behind chaos.

During my second year some students let me read their humanities and history papers—poems, essays, epitaphs, and fiction. Much of their poetry and prose was eloquent and expressed their fears and yearning to learn:

"Black Women"

Black women, black women,
why are you crying?

Black men, black men,
why are you dying?

Black people, black people
don't ever stop trying!

Unite black people for
we are all one.

Prosper black family
the power will come.

> *Educate our people and*
> *know where you're from.*
>
> *Determination and salvation*
> *is all you really need.*
>
> *Love your black people*
> *for we are God's seed.*
>
> *We feel the oppressor and*
> *we don't feel freed.*
>
> *Be strong, for we are the beginning.*
> *Be strong, for we are black women.*
>
> — *Landa B.*

My sense about a classical education was confirmed by John Richey, the teacher in charge of the computer room, a very caring mentor who loved the kids and was unusually patient and supportive. John told me about a game he played with the kids that revealed their true skills:

We brainstormed to build a better bathtub. They came up with incredible ideas. Instead of having the water go in the tub and sit there, you have spigots all around. The water would be constantly sucked out and recycled, so water is not sitting there. Getting fresh water all the time. Self-cleaning bathtubs. Vibrating bathtubs. A soft surface for the tub, like putty, that would respond to your body.

A problem that doesn't require academic background, taps into their creativity. As teachers, we are still bound by reading and writing and texts. And they are not; that's not their skill. I said, "Think about something and respond. I want a lot of quick ideas." Glenn suggested knobs that would be breasts. Kareem talked about naked girls. Our kids are verbally adept. We should begin with their oral skills—do interviews, tell stories. The challenge is to go from their oral skills—tell stories, do interviews—back to the written word.

Having abandoned *A People's History*, I wanted to locate some major event, more or less contemporary, that was recorded as oral history, an event in which the evidence and the context suggested many plausible interpretations. The Cuban missile crisis came to mind, in part because the Kennedy Library has created a wonderful resource for students— Kennedy recordings of the Executive Committee in the Oval Office; memos from McGeorge Bundy, Secretary of Defense Robert S. McNamara, Secretary of State Dean Rusk, Arthur Schlesinger, and others; reports and advice from the Joint Chiefs; correspondence between Kennedy and Khrushchev, and Khrushchev and Castro; photos of the missiles taken from the air; and an oral history with Dean Acheson. These were the kinds of conversations the kids could sympathize with, a dialectic of life and death between the two most powerful gangs in the world. The missile crisis was a metaphor for life in the ghetto with its conflagrations and outbursts of violence.

The crisis offered us an unusual opportunity to study uncertainty and how easy it is to draw false conclusions that seem perfectly reasonable. It gave us a chance to think about options, all based on more or less incorrect or insufficient information. Our work was about Kennedy and Khrushchev's dilemma and our own. It was about thinking clearly, thinking about life and death, thinking about what brought the world to this point.

The class, titled "First Person History," originally had two small sections, one of which quickly disappeared. Students came and went. I appointed one student in each section to note the major points we made and the vocabulary we missed and another student to record the facts we did not know. We reviewed these the following week.

"First Person History" was an elective and therefore met only one hour a week. This turned out to be a major drawback. By the time we began to role-play and to look seriously into the problems Kennedy confronted, the hour was over. The following week we had to review and begin again. I asked the principal for relief, but there was no additional time available. We shared Thursday morning at 11:15 with yoga, Tai Chi, parenting, Spanish, and newspaper.

There was a tremendous difference between my first try using *A People's History of the United States*, a much larger class, and this tutorial. The situation this time was intimate, everyone at the same table, eye to eye, a sense of common enterprise, no hierarchy, more camaraderie, fewer barriers. It was difficult to "leave" the room mentally because everyone was called on every few minutes. Participation became contagious. The kids in "First Person History" were "with" me.

Jorge attended about half the time, but he was so bright that he could grasp the positions taken by McNamara, Rusk, Bundy, and the others by listening to bits and pieces of tape. But he really didn't care about school and wouldn't follow through. His business was intellectual pyrotechnics and self-promotion. He responded as long as he was the center of attention. Like so many kids at Egleston, Jorge suffered from low self-esteem, the foundation, I assume, for his nihilistic view of the world. His insecurities crippled his intelligence, which was considerable, and made him a sad clown. He didn't believe he could think because he didn't believe in himself. And he didn't believe in himself because those around him were struggling for their own selfhood. So it was perfectly all right with me for our class to shower attention on Jorge. He needed it. I noticed, however, that Jorge always managed to avoid reading. He passed memoranda to the next person. He excused himself when his time came. He was absent on the day he was to role-play McNamara. He feigned laryngitis. I learned late in the term that Jorge was severely dyslexic and unfortunately very much ashamed of it. He had reached his senior year in high school, and no one in the Boston Public School System had diagnosed his dyslexia.

At Egleston, brutal reality, illusion, and secrets abound. Girls are in their sixth month of pregnancy, and no one knows. Boys go to school in the morning and sell crack and heroin in the afternoon. Some kids, maddened by sexual abuse, limp through school without effect. Many grieve for the dead, their bereavement hidden by weed. I did not know until later that Marieca was a severe alcoholic, or that one boy had shot and wounded another, or that Angela had children. The school has girls who are regularly beaten by their boyfriends and who pretend that they have found true love:

"Survivor of Domestic Violence"

What is it like to be a survivor of domestic violence?
What is it like when your boyfriend walks in and you're terrified instead of happy?

What is it like when you go to sleep at night and you think somebody's watching you?
You look again but there's nobody there.
You walk down the street with him, and people are looking at you,
Because they can see in your face something's wrong.

What is it like when you're on the train and you repeatedly get screamed at?
What is it like living in fear that your child will be kidnapped?
What is it like to think he might decide to kill you today?
I don't think you know unless you've been a victim yourself.

What is it like when you tell someone your problems and
all they say is get out.

They think it's easy.
What is it like to wish you were dead before your
boyfriend lays another hand on you,
Burns you with a lighter, or tries to suffocate you with
a pillow?
Think about it.

Maybe he might come over and be nice for a while.
You make him a nice hot grilled cheese sandwich
And he decides he doesn't like it, so he
scrubs your face with it.
You have to be a victim of domestic violence to
understand.
What is it like when the baby is scared of him and
because she won't let him feed her,
He beats you with the baby's bottle until your arm is
black and blue.
What is it like to be a survivor of domestic violence?
You probably don't know.

What is it like to live like this for a whole year?
Not good at all, you're really not living.

— Evelyn Alicia

The alternative urban high school does not have pupils. It has warriors, survivors, teenage mothers, alcoholics, dealers, sexually abused kids, depressives. It has kids who are invariably high and kids who are twenty but read as if they were twelve. The imprint of this suffering obliterates the pupil. School may be the avenue of last resort, but many kids at Egleston believe it leads nowhere. There are few good jobs. A future of minimum-wage employment does not make school an attractive passage.

How do you expect me to study? I work two jobs in a hospital and a restaurant, twelve hours a day. I work in housekeeping and sometimes in the kitchen. It's better for me to sleep because where does school lead to? There are no jobs—computer operator fixer—but you know, Murray, what faces us? Nothing. Shit jobs, fast-food jobs? What's a black man or Hispanic going to do? They got us hemmed in, man. We are their junk heap. We are the cheap labor they need.

We are dealing with special kids, kids who find school alien and useless, kids who secretly wish to fail. But we are also dealing with kids who want to know why they are poor and last. I spent three years at Egleston trying to help them find real answers.

God, I can't go to history. It is so boring. I can't stand it. We don't study stuff that has anything to do with my life. Why don't they talk about the real things. Why are we poor? Why do we kill each other? Why don't we get anywhere? Who owns our houses and stores, and how did they get it, and how do we get it back? These are the real questions. That's what they should teach. Now you see why school is Mickey Mouse.

Michelle's sentiments are widely shared. For many, school is just another alienating experience, a mock effort to elevate them in a world that really has no place for them. Michelle described the high school she attended before Egleston:

Most of the time we read a few pages from some dumb story and then had to write a summary of it. It was stupid. And it had nothing to do with my life, our life. Yeah, there was little stories about Hispanics and blacks who made it, became doctors or engineers, but there was something phony about it. Where will we be ten years from now? Dead or making shit in McDonald's. The teachers didn't care. They just wanted to get rid of us.

The kids in "First Person History" didn't want to be insulted by stupid work. They wanted to know. They wanted to be stretched. They wanted to see their imagination pay off. The kids often talked about the high school they attended before Egleston. The story was basically the same—rote learning, angry teachers, boredom alleviated by disruptions or drugs or alcohol. There were occasional variations, a wonderful teacher now and then, an interesting course on occasion, but the theme never varied: school had nothing to do with life, teachers were racist, and what difference did it make? No one had a future.

I hated it, that's why I left. The classes were too big. The teacher never knew who I was. A number surrounded by other numbers. Who cares about the story of young white boys or girls? It has nothing to do with me. The teachers wanted to get out as fast as possible. I didn't learn nothing. I'm Hispanic, not American. American history has nothing to do with me. Your friend Zinn shows—what's the name of the book we studied, yeah, *People's History*—shows how the Europeans murdered us and really enslaved us, what a bastard Columbus was. That was for me. It meant something to me. But not the shit we studied in high school.

I asked Robert one day why he had left high school for Egleston:

I didn't leave. They threw me out. I hated it. It was boring. The work was stupid. It seemed to me that when I was a freshman, we were doing sixth- or seventh-grade work. And when I was a junior, we did the same stuff as the eighth grade. I used to finish the assignments in twenty minutes, so I used to leave, and I got in trouble.

Robert later talked about the "photograph" white teachers have of their black students:

This photograph never changes despite how good you are in school. So what happens is you never get rewarded, never get a good grade, and you give up, not give up, get worse, disrupt. It's like a child who never gets love from his mama, what's going to happen? He is going to hate himself, he thinks he is to blame; and when he grows up, he hates himself, he will do drugs and crime, and he will hate his mother. The whole thing, the family, the gang, the school, held together by caring. And that's what we don't have.

Egleston is life and death, eros and thanatos, a passion to live and be free and a retreat from life, a melancholy stifling of the urge to live after loving friends have been murdered. Every day every teacher tries to excite the dead, to convince them that there is something beautiful about history or math. One of the most experienced teachers has been coping with this grief for years:

It's very rare when a student responds with excitement or really cares. These kids carry a history of defeat. It's a monotone, affectless. I think it would be great if they could find a way to talk about it. The muteness is a response to the horrors of their life. They can't talk about those kids who were killed. They can't think about it, the grief, the horror. School is a way to take their mind off this grief. Maybe if they could get that out, they could get beyond it and deal with what's happening. It's not just the grief of losing friends—it's the grief of being fatherless, the grief of being poor, the grief of their whole life. That's why they need things that are fast-moving—video games, television, rap—stuff that will take them away. This is a big reason why they can't do what we did in school—read books, write papers. The rhythm is not right.

"Open Up"

Every hood got youngstas who got it bad
so open up before we end up in a bodybag
And when we do your hearts will be broken up
Open up, we've had centuries of bad luck
Look what my generation is facing
Life or death trying to dodge incarceration.

— *Demitri Robertson*

I chose the Cuban missile crisis because the rhythm was right. It was the ultimate video. Kennedy and Khrushchev were the metaphor in which the kids could see danger, violence, and the contemplation of death. I thought this potential holocaust would engage everyone.

Although Marieca, Robert, and Jorge did well in class, the experiment was not a complete success. Other students in "First Person History"— Kathy, Cynthia, Shavon, William, Jose—were often absent. Cynthia—a stately Latino girl with vivid brown eyes, classic features, a large open smile that seemed to me to betray a prior and more joyous existence— was frequently beaten by her drug-dealer boyfriend. She was more concerned with her physical safety than with analyzing McNamara's memo to Kennedy. She was a perfect example of the double life so many of the kids live. It was hard to tell whether I was talking to Kathy, the student at Egleston, or Kathy the girl who was abused by her mother for years and who jumped with fright when I pounded on the table. She would disappear for a week or two. The social worker remarked myste-riously, "Kathy is having a hard time."

William had been a student of mine before. He was a member of that army of black youths who are depressed and mute, secretly angry but always polite, one of the boys who resides in some distant land where there is less pain. William could not cope with our class; he was unable to mobilize enough energy to read a single assignment. He came once in a while, muttered, role-played without showing any internal feeling. He was present but absent. He hid behind a frozen face and a jacket pulled high around his neck. I tried, cajoled, provided the relevant facts, told William where we were and where we were going, and then I lost control: "God damn it, what's wrong with you? Wake up! You are not dumb! You have a good mind. You have survived for twenty years in this shitty neighborhood. You have street smarts. It's just one step to school smarts. You can tell me what Khrushchev's position was. Read it again." William was still far away from us. He sat silently as if in some catatonic state. "I don't know," he said.

"Here Is Something You Can't Understand"

What is it like to be herbed?
Some say pure bliss.
Some feel confusion.
What do I say to this?
I say you feel like you're in your own world,
that no one else can understand
if they're not herbed.

The ultimate high cannot be controlled.
Your head is spinning so fast
you feel dizzy.
Your heart is pounding so hard
and racing so fast
You are sure it's going to just
Pop
and
leave you lying
helplessly . . .

in the place where
you're standing.
It's just your imagination, no, your intoxication,
*   deceiving your psyche again.*

But don't get me wrong, it is quite a joy to do what
*   I want and not be annoyed.*
Bob my head to some music
or think to myself,
But I'm scared when I talk,
I can't control my mouth.
I chatter on and on once I start,
and I say some stupid shit,
but after I'm done I ask myself if I really said it.
You see, there's no borderline between my mind
*   and what's real.*
I can do what I want.
I have nothing to fear.

Here is something you can't understand . . .
When I'm in my own Candyland.
In a psychedelic world where paranoia is near
There are no visions of gumdrops,
but gunshots in the air.
But sometimes I'd rather be herbed
than to fear what I fear.

But being herbed has its own set of fears,
"Who's watching me now, I can feel a cold stare!
But when I turn around, there's nobody there.
It's just the indonesia,
my brain teaser,
teasing my senses again.

To be herbed is a delight,
It is also your right.

It's a time when you can relax.
It's a time when you can bug.
It's a time to think to yourself.
Most of all it's a time when you don't have standards.
What it's like for me to be herbed?
I can tell you this,
It's a time when I can get some things accomplished.

One hit of the Boodah,
Two tokes of a Blizz
and I'm up and going
to deal with my biz'.
How could this motivate me, some might ask . . .
Like I said, it helps me to relax.
If you have not begun,
and were too scared to have began,
Then like I've said,
you won't understand.

So for those who don't know
"Ya betta' ask somebody,"
but as for me I already know.
But now I must go,
And play tic-tac-toe
Down a row of homies
To see who got the Phillies . . .
but if they're puffin, not for nothin,
"Where the dub at, fool?"
I reply, "Show me some lute and I'll put
you
down
too!"
                              — Nytia N. Porter

Most of the kids in class were political illiterates. Barbara O'Hearn, who had been teaching in the Boston system for twenty years, a very hard-headed woman who cared deeply for her students, appraised their intellectual inventory:

They have no politics, or for that matter no serious views about anything because they don't know anything outside of their immediate experience, and I mean anything. They don't read books. Very few read newspapers, and from what they tell me, neither do their parents. They have no support groups, no models, no encouragement. They have no one except teachers urging them to read. Their culture, like most American kids', is visual. They are educated by television.

Only one student knew who Castro was. And Jorge, a Cuban expatriate, was the only student who knew where Cuba was located. Kathy placed it in Spain, Cynthia in Canada. No one had heard of the Cold War or Khrushchev or the missile crisis. No one could name anything that any American president since Lincoln had done except Jorge, who knew that Clinton advocated a health bill. One student knew there had been a Civil War. No one knew where Philadelphia or Ohio was located. Only Marieca and Robert could name an event connected with Martin Luther King, Jr. No one could locate Panama or the Suez Canal. One student had heard of FDR. No one was sure whether more Democrats or more Republicans opposed abortion. One student supplied the following information:

I told you the number of Jews in the United States is sixty million, more than people think. Russia is three times us ... two hundred million and we be seventy million. Blacks in America about half, about sixty million. I can't tell you exactly where France and England are, but I know they are in Europe.

These gaps made it difficult, probably impossible, to understand much about the history taught in high school. It was impossible for us to develop any sophisticated argument because the terms were missing. The sense of place and time and the issues that frame historical events were absent. Miriam, who joined our class during the second semester, for example, knew several facts, but most of them were scrambled, and she didn't know what many of them meant:

I know a lot about the missile crisis. It was October 1962. America and Russia in a Cold War. Russia sends missiles to Cuba. Both are communist, I know, but I don't know what communist means. Khrushchev was head of Russia. Cuba had, I think, we study so far, fourteen missiles and some of them are many feet long and many feet wide. You ask, what is Russia trying to accomplish? I don't know. They easy to transport so they sent a lot. I don't know why Russia wants all this trouble. We do what we do, and they do what they do.

The students could not talk about a serious topic except in the most primitive terms, a kind of baby talk:

Why did Khrushchev send the missiles to Cuba? He wanted to. He likes to cause trouble. Because he is Russian. He like the Cubans. They asked him to, and he is a friend. Why shouldn't he? He has so many he won't miss them. He is doing them a favor. It was not expensive for him to do this. He can't lose anything. That's why he did it. I don't know. Why shouldn't he send missiles to Cuba? A lot of people do.

It took me some months to understand the subtleties that sometimes actually lay behind this talk. In this case, Khrushchev's actions were described as if he were the leader of a giant gang that found pleasure in provocation, a gang lord bound by ties of friendship, loyal to the final moment, but also a gang man who understood that the cost was low and there was little to lose. The missile crisis was a calculated rumble.

We began to listen to the tapes Kennedy made of conversations in the Oval Office. The audio was a bit fuzzy because the president kept his recorder in a desk drawer to avoid detection. But you could hear McNamara, Rusk, Bundy, General Taylor, et al. No one in the class had ever heard of the missile crisis or Khrushchev.

I talked about the Cold War and the arrival of the missiles in Cuba for about thirty minutes and then asked, "If you were President Kennedy, what would you do?" Robert and Marieca immediately suggested three of the six alternatives that had actually been considered: an invasion of Cuba, air strikes against the missile bases, and negotiation. Jorge shared the bellicose sentiments of many Cuban exiles: "Bomb the shit out of Cuba. Get rid of Castro and the missiles at the same time." Marieca, clairvoyant, suggested that we trade any missiles we might have near Russia for the missiles in Cuba. Kathy, who had been silent, added an option, "Invade Cuba. We have the big army; we have the planes. They have nothing. Why not just capture Cuba, get rid of the missiles, bring 'em back to the U.S.? It would be simple."

The tape was difficult to understand. We switched to the typescript, but the kids became frustrated by so much reading. They unleashed a billingsgate against the schools and their own impotence:

How I'm going to understand this? I don't know what they talk about. I don't know what Khrushchev wants or who he is. I don't even know where Cuba is. I'm not even sure where Europe is or Asia. What happened to me, to my school? Why didn't they teach me these things? Why am I ignorant? I feel stupid. I'm angry. We don't know shit. I am not stupid, but I don't know. That's why I don't speak up in class. I am ashamed. They don't teach the real stuff, and those white teachers don't like us. I'm goin' to learn. I goin' to talk in class even if it looks wrong. The schools not teaching us. It's part of the whole thing in America to make sure we're ignorant. And if we be ignorant, they got us and use us. We gotta learn. That's how we get out.

You dumb niggers. They control the schools. They control us. But we got a chance here. Josh and Murray and Beth [all teachers] maybe are different. They tells us the truth. Somehow they got in the system without being noticed. We can learn from them, no bullshit here. We got to study how the dudes on top runs things. Maybe our missile crisis will tell us. These are the guys on top. So if we listen to them talk, we got something.

When I pointed out that the president considered the options they mentioned everyone applauded—lots of high fives. Classes at Egleston often begin in silence and then comes an explosion—staccato answers, often intuitive, often crazy, no details, no context, no argument. Their first response is bombastic:

Bomb the shit out of Russia. We must have thousands of missiles, you said we did. And we got missiles near Russia, so why don't we nuclearize them? No one can beat us. Nuke 'em, nuke 'em.

The culture of *now* discourages negotiation and promotes direct action. A status system based on respect and instant retaliation does not produce diplomats. The same kids who despise America and believe the country is killing them with AIDS rally to the flag when America is threatened. Jorge says, "We're number one." The others agree. This kind of jingoism indicates just how successfully America is being sold to minority kids, who talk a lot about how phoney the American dream is but remain steadfast consumers:

What if Russia attacked? We'll get them first. They could not be as strong as we are. Their missiles probably are not as good as ours. We're first, number one, we can really make things. We'll teach them who to respect—

bam, bam. Hit 'em first, ask questions later. That's how many kids here live, and it works.

Then came a more practical reaction:

You dumb nigger. What you think Russia is goin' to do? Watch? Wait? No, they goin' to send their missiles to us, and they destroy New York and Boston and Washington. So think before you nuke someone. You got to think about consequences, about what the other side be. Be they big and powerful, you can't just bomb people without expecting they hit you back. It's the scene in the hood. Only pick on little guys, or have your gun ready. Maybe nobody shoot nuclear because both sides afraid of, what's that word, retaliation. Yeah, that's it, retaliation.

Teaching social science at Egleston requires establishing the entire terrain: noting large numbers of facts, defining the relevant geography, presenting the history, talking about what constitutes a cause and an effect, defining context, and explaining what it means to truly understand an event—that is, stressing the process of becoming. My emphasis was not on teaching dates, facts, and names, but on process, change, dialectic, conflict, and becoming. The issue in our tutorial was always *why*. *Why* was Kennedy concerned with Europe's good will? *Why* did JFK not agree with his more militant advisers? *Why* did Khrushchev send missiles to Cuba in the first place? How did misinformation affect decision making? How and why did people and nations move to their destiny? What were the tensions that would produce any resolution? Could the outcome have been different? The point was always daily life in the neighborhood, why one student got shot, why his best friend was doing well in junior college. Teaching at Egleston means showing how the actions of one friend or enemy can inadvertantly change the behavior of another:

It's easy to suggest that we bomb Cuba, or invade, or negotiate. But what about Russia, what will Russia do? America does not live in a vacuum, and neither do you. You are limited by the actions of others, they affect you, and the U.S. is limited by Russia's arms and power. Each nation affects the other. Each of you affects the other and all uncertain outcomes. Your power is always limited. And a lot of unpredictable things happen. Think about the possible consequences of your actions.

To predict what Russia will do, or America, don't we have to know where they are coming from and where they want to get to? Would it help if I told you that the United States invaded Russia in 1917? The U.S. invaded Cuba, Russia's friend. Got to think about the history of these places, the baggage they bring. You've got to think about the consequences of each option—the context.

During our early meetings, most of the students thought only of direct action and instant retaliation. The students had trouble thinking about consequences or even considering what Russia might do. Their myopia, I think, was culturally induced. For them, the United States and Cuba were the only antagonists. They never thought about the reaction of any other country. It was as if the world were bipolar, two countries, two street fighters, two gangs. These kids rarely leave the neighborhood. Everything, the universe, is here and now or, at most, a few miles away. Their parochialism has produced a spatial and temporal tunnel vision.

The kids often mistook the existence of something for its cause and rarely thought abstractly. I asked Cynthia what the significance is of the fact that we know the Russian missiles are x feet long and y feet in diameter. She replied, "Well, they are x feet long and y feet in diameter." William and Jorge would repeat questions as if the act of repetition converted the question into an answer: "Why did Khrushchev send missiles to Cuba?" "Because he wanted missiles in Cuba." "What did he plan to do with the missiles?" "Whatever he wanted to do." "Why do Kennedy and Khrushchev write each other—actually by wireless telegram?" "Because they are good writers, and they like to make their thoughts open to the public. There is no way to talk to Russia. I'm sure they got no phones in those days between the two."

I presented the crisis as JFK saw it, an international puzzle, a chess game with horrendous consequences, but a game we could play in retrospect and with pleasure. I described the missile crisis as potentially the most dangerous event in our history. I described the likely effects of a nuclear bomb landing in Miami or Dallas: millions dead, a gigantic fire storm, excruciating death through radiation. I quoted the famous remark that the living would envy the dead. Everyone was absolutely dumbfounded, speechless, and then came the incredulity, the defense against reality: "I don't believe any bomb could kill millions of people. It just can't be that strong. Some people will live and start again."

Robert and the others knew the stakes. They knew they were dealing with something cataclysmic, and this was an important reason why they became involved. The students were interested in a world of life-and-death matters, because that is what they knew:

These dudes had the same problems we do. What to do when you suddenly meet some dude from the projects who wants to kill you—hide, ambush, shoot, get away, get him later when he's not ready. There is not much time. You have to think fast and do. I've been in this situation.

So have I, many days. You turn a corner, and there is some crazy guy, out of his skull, pointing a gun at you. You know, like Khrushchev, a very big gun. And the guy is drunk or high, it's obvious, like Khrushchev, who is drunk with the idea of bringing Kennedy down, or America, so what do you do? Not much time to decide. So you look at the dude and try to figure out who he is, what he'll do, what you call alternatives—your phrase, process information. All very quick and very dangerous. And I don't have missiles like Kennedy did.

Robert's talk about the dangers of the street was prophetic. He was wounded six times in a drive-by shooting by a gang from a rival housing project while he was leaving his mother's house. He survived, returned to school for a month, and then was asked to leave because he had not fulfilled his contract. He was readmitted, disappeared, and then permanently suspended for absenteeism and failure to work.

We continued to read the transcripts of the discussion recorded in Kennedy's office on October 16, 1962. The students in "First Person History" had never read primary sources, and they were bothered by the broken speech and interruptions. They did not know who any of the participants were except Kennedy, and the only thing they knew about him was that he was president. No one knew when he had been president; they guessed the 1970s or 1980s. No one knew who Lyndon Johnson was. Two students located Russia above Canada, and no one knew where France or Brazil or Egypt or China was located. We needed a basic geography lesson.

I expected little response to our geography lesson. I was wrong. The lesson turned out to be one of the most exciting hours we spent. As I located countries and the great oceans and rivers on the map, and presented the rudiments of economic geography and military power, the kids in "First Person History" seemed to recover the enthusiasm of eight-year-olds watching a magic bazaar full of treats and amazing tricks. Robert and Marieca, masters of realpolitik in the hood, couldn't stop talking:

Now you can see why Russia sends missiles to Cuba. Look how close Cuba is—ninety miles—and look how far away Russia is. But look at how big Russia is. They got the oil and the metals. Look at the area Murray showed that the missiles could destroy. The South, the whole South. I got cousins there. Russia be smart to send Cuba missiles. But look at these canals, Panama. I don't remember the other one—Suez, Suez. Look at the miles you can save. How do they build canals? I want to know how those canals work.

No wonder America and England kept them. That's the whole story. The big countries kill the little ones. That's always the way it is. No wonder the blacks in Africa were captured. Only two things count—who has guns and who has food and oil. Either you got this, or you force other countries to give or sell.

Robert's view of the world reflected his life in his neighborhood. He led our class, but we had other kids who spoke only when spoken to and then reluctantly. Kathy rarely talked, I think, because she was afraid of looking ridiculous, afraid she didn't know anything, afraid she would be mocked by colleagues and yelled at by teachers. She, like so many of our students, had suffered multiple wounds that could be healed only by some success and the patient encouragement of teachers and friends. The injured at Egleston defended themselves by hating school or believing it was irrelevant or by playing dumb. But periodically they revealed the intelligence and the yearning that lie behind the wounds. Miriam, who joined us later, gave a little disquisition on economic geography:

But the important geography is economic geography. That is more important than the size of a country. Who got oil and copper and metals. You can be big like China, but no machines, no industry, too many people, and you got little. And small like Arabia, with a lot of oil and lots of power.

Marieca and Robert couldn't stop. Here were two very tough smart street kids, one addicted to liquor, the other a scam artist and a periodic dealer in cocaine and heroin, excited by geography, talking about oil and exploitation. They spoke as if they had discovered these countries and were the first to speculate about geopolitics. It was amazing and beautiful, a marvelous demonstration of the excitement generated by learning something grand. But there was also a strong sense of deprivation:

The mountains and rivers must have been important in history. The mountains stopped enemies and the rivers could be used to send troops or food or anything. Think if you have mountains and rivers, look, America and Russia have both.

Marieca suddenly stopped talking and became angry:

Why we never learn this in the high school we come from? It's important to know geography. You can't talk about history or politics or economics without knowing where the rivers are and the countries. Robert, we been robbed. We be entitled to know just as much as kids in the suburbs. I never heard about what Murray teaches, and nobody ever told me to look for causes and effects and what you call the context.

Robert assured everyone that their ignorance was the result of a conspiracy to disempower minorities:

They didn't teach us because they don't want us to know. They want us to be ignorant so they can control us—not knowing is one of the best ways they do this. There are two sets of teachers, one for white kids, and they learn, and one for us. Murray told us thought is a weapon, more powerful than guns. We don't have that weapon. And since we turned off from school, we ain't going to get that weapon.

I hoped that geopolitics would lead them to think about power and powerlessness in the neighborhood, and it did. As I said in the beginning,

I wanted to radicalize the kids at Egleston. I wanted them to get to the roots of their lives. To do this, they had to recognize their servitude and their ignorance. Most Egleston kids don't think about these things. But the students in "First Person History" were becoming angry, feeling cheated by the schools, robbed of something they were entitled to. And the more they discovered what they didn't know, the more they wanted to know. I think they realized that the missile crisis was a tremendous event and that they needed to know much more. The dialectic between Kennedy and Khrushchev was a natural segue to their struggles. They were beginning to see that reason is a very powerful weapon and that ignorance and impotence go hand in hand.

Robert's speech is a lament about the ignorance and impotence of black kids. It is also a demand for good teachers and meaningful work. To some degree, Robert is right: there are two sets of teachers. The ghetto repels and the suburbs attract. Tracking is not merely a technique to separate students; it also describes the unspoken and self-selected process by which teachers gravitate to more easily controllable and diligent students in the suburbs and away from "unruly" minorities in dangerous cities. There are thousands of exceptions, but Robert's observation is basically true. Academic apartheid exists.

That Thursday was a thrilling day for me. The kids in "First Person History" were amazed by geography when it was taught in ways they could relate to: the sources of power and powerlessness among nations (food, oil, minerals, waterways, mountains, manpower, technologies). The students recognized the complex relations between geography and politics, and they were excited when they realized that conflict in the hood was also a matter of geopolitics.

Of course, not all the students were as engaged as Robert and Marieca. The geography lesson had less effect on the others, who had a very sketchy idea of the Cold War one week after I had discussed it and were unable to identify several countries in Europe after our geography lesson.

The students are not responsible for their monumental lack of information, but the handicap is staggering. Kathy, for example, insisted that Cuba was in Canada because it was in the Western hemisphere. How could she understand the missile crisis? Fortunately, all these facts can be taught, and very effectively, if teachers excite students and show that the missile crisis and the Suez Canal are wonders, part of a great chain that reaches back and has relevance to them. The desire to learn geography and history will follow:

I think I know what you are doing here. The missile business is like our business, like what's going in the hood. You got gangs, two gangs, Russia and America, both got a long history of hate and revenge, like the projects here, and both plan to destroy the other.

Before we began, none of the students knew anything about the Cold War, so the Cuban missile crisis appeared to them as an alien, abstract "no contest" between a pygmy and a giant, a struggle between a powerful gang and an upstart, a pseudo-event without any point:

What's the crisis? We destroy them. Who is going to do anything about it? Nobody would dare hit us. So there is no crisis. Don't countries send guns to each other all the time, and don't they join and play games all the time—bang, bang, I'll kill you if you don't give me the ball? And countries fake all the time, and that's what all of this is about, threat and fake. We do this all the time on the street.

Jorge has delivered a strange but not unusual scenario for Egleston— shrewd and intuitive insights based on his own experience coupled with incorrect facts. His theory of realpolitik is accurate, but he also believes the missile crisis was nothing to get upset about.

The perspective of the students in class was framed by what I call apocalyptic instant history. Their everyday life has been a life pock-marked by sudden cataclysm. Their perspective is biblical, sober, and vengeful. The *Lex Taliones* is their code: an eye for an eye and a tooth for a tooth. Their history is chaotic and supercharged—sex for boys at eleven, babies for girls at sixteen. For these kids, art imitates life. "N.Y.P.D. Blue," "Law and Order," "E.R.," and "Chicago Hope" confirm and extend their world with a menu of violence, death, danger, and occasional redemption. Life is a series of fragments for these kids, fitful nonsequitors held together by a tenuous thread of survival. Their personal history is episodic and catastrophic, and so is their view of history.

There is nothing that Kennedy can do except obliterate Cuba and Russia with nuclear weapons. He should have done it right away, as soon as he got the word. Why not? Get them by surprise like the Japs did. This is what the world's about—respect and power. A guy looks at me the wrong way, swear at me, call me a son of a bitch—bang, it's over. I don't ask questions.

Their remembrance of things past, like that of most adolescents in America, extends to last week or perhaps last month. In class, their responses invariably had to do with current events unfettered by context. They had little sense that the acts of one nation affect the response of others. They treated actions as if they were isolated and discreet:

Look, these countries speak different languages, right? And they live by themselves. They are their own boss. Their government does what it wants to do. Until there is a war, and then one country can affect another. But they are so far apart, thousands of miles, that they are their own boss. So you study one country at a time.

Instant history placed few limitations on the imagination of the students in our class, a situation that encouraged some novel insights. Marieca, for example, suggested at our first meeting that the United States buy the missiles in Cuba. "Let's buy the missiles in Cuba and end it. Everything's for sale. Why not missiles? They probably need the money. Everything has a price." No one familiar with the history of the Cold War would suggest a sale. The context of Cuban, Russian, American relations precluded this solution. But in Marieca's world, the sale of illicit material is taken for granted. Cocaine is for sale, weed is for sale, credit cards are for sale, prostitutes are for sale, the police are for sale. Why not Cuban missiles?

Marieca's suggestion is a beautiful example of how historical ignorance and local culture join to produce surreal views of the world, a kind of Egleston Square history writ large. In the absence of any clear idea of the past, local custom is elevated to universal history. But there is a strangely true aspect to Marieca's suggestion because in fact America has been "buying" countries for many years. The CIA bankrolled right-wing Japanese parties for decades and has purchased dozens of anticommunist regimes since the 1950s. Marieca doesn't know these facts but still provides insight into American foreign policy. Her understanding is of an America stripped of amenities, reduced to the purest Darwinian terms. Marieca's views are profoundly American: the country is a shopping mall, everything is for sale.

Though the missile crisis resonated in their lives, my students nevertheless had to immerse themselves into the thinking of white-elite America to understand the missile crisis. This task required a tremendous leap of imagination. They had to feel the alien vocabulary and logic of Kennedy and his colleagues. They had to enter the heads of American businessmen and generals and Russian politicians. Marieca told me that she felt we were learning several languages at once:

We've got to know all these words we've never seen and all those places, Turkey and the like, and the history. And then we got to think in a new way, logic and strategy. My head gets ruffled up. I get confused thinking about all this stuff at one time. It's easy to get mixed up.

I understood and sympathized. There was a great deal going on, and it was totally new. I tried to clarify things by relating Kennedy's dilemma to theirs.

You must remember that Kennedy and Khrushchev are being watched by their armies, and the public, and by people who want to see them fail, people who want to take over. And they have to decide which groups they want to please and how far they are willing to anger other groups. Do you think about your parents when you are about to make a big move, or your girlfriend, or the gang? Does the gang make you do things you don't want to? What about your conscience, your sense of right and wrong, and your religion. Does that affect you?

For the second time, a student suggested we buy the missiles from Cuba. "We go down there, give 'em a good price. After all, missiles probably cost a lot, and this is a serious situation." Everybody laughed.

She's got a good idea. They're poor like we are in Roxbury. Those Cubans won't be able to resist a good price. Poor people are forced to sell when they can. Maybe, probably, we could bribe the Russians, they ain't so rich. I bet Khrushchev has a price, all politicians do. The world ain't so different from us—buy and sell. Money, Murray, money is what makes things go. Think of how we be if we had money. Buying the missiles is not so dumb.

We had analyzed about thirty pages of the October 16th transcript when I asked, "What would be the advantage of negotiating with

Khrushchev?" Kathy was having trouble with the vocabulary and, I thought, was having trouble making sense out of so many arguments. She replied, "Less will die. The U.S. will not be destroyed. Russia won't bomb. We probably don't need the missiles in Turkey anyway. It's the best way to do this." These had been the sentiments of Kennedy's more pacific advisers. Kathy had little interest in school, little hope for the future, but she had uncommon common sense.

The result of years in the Boston system was a massive collective ignorance and hatred of school. Many Egleston students were restless. Despite their loyalty when America was threatened by Russia, they did not feel proud of the United States or nourished by its myths of well-being. I tried to imagine what the Cuban missile crisis or all the other things we talked about meant to them. I was rarely sure whom I was talking to at Egleston because very little seemed to be stable or transparent. Conversations that seemed clear to me, I later discovered, meant something entirely different to a student. I would say, "The homework is Chapter 4 in Zinn's book—twenty pages for the week." They would say, "I lost the book," "I forgot my book," "the print was too small," "reading so much is too hard." To me, the assignment was a way station to a different life, a step to self-realization. To some students, it was an intrusion or an impossibility. We were not coming to this task from the same place.

Kathy and the others began to understand some of the dimensions of the missile crisis by the fifth or sixth week. Kathy grasped the advantages of negotiating. She was beginning to think critically. She understood that the loss of Turkish missiles would not have seriously hurt America's offensive capability. She knew we had missiles at other sites. She was concerned with the safety of the United States, and she understood that negotiation could preempt a Russian attack. I asked her after class why America really didn't need missiles in Turkey, and she told me, "Because America had many other missiles sites, so why not use

Turkey to bargain? Russia wants to get rid of Turkish missiles. They want this. We can make a good trade and not really lose anything." By our seventh meeting, four of the kids in "First Person History" were beginning to think about consequences. They were using information to infer: "We know the height and how wide. We can compare this with photos of the May Day parade in Moscow and tell what kind of missile and then how far it will shoot." On occasion, they used historical context to predict:

Khrushchev got a good point here. We invaded Russia in 1917. We invaded his friend Cuba. We have an illegal blockade. Khrushchev is not going to forgive this. He will not surrender. History tells him what he must do.

They were beginning to realize that many constituencies were involved: "You must remember that Kennedy and Khrushchev are being watched by their armies and the public." Half the class was thinking about relationships and political dynamics. I thought our progress was unusual.

Kathy understood the principle of deterrence and distinguished appearance from reality. Remember that this was a girl who had been abused by her mother for years, a girl with little sense of self-worth. Like the others, Kathy had never heard of the missile crisis or read a single work of nonfiction outside of school. She read slowly. Her vocabulary was poor. But she was willing to take a chance. I was thrilled by her answer. At Egleston, small triumphs can become landmarks. I needed some sign that the kids were beginning to understand, and Kathy gave it to me.

The talk about bombing Cuba disappeared around the fifth week. I asked the class, "When two sides have equal firepower, what is the most likely outcome?" José, who joined us during the third week, immediately replied, "Neither side is likely to attack the other because each one can destroy the other. So a lot of arms on both sides, which looks bad, is good, is for peace. Each side has time to fire back." José's cogency surprised us. But after this initial contribution, José retired from the class, hiding behind some sadness or fear. I had to coax José, reassure him. And then, after my courtship, he would on occasion answer in a tiny, sparrow-like voice, a miniwhisper that made me wonder what had strangled this boy's life. José stayed with us for four weeks and disappeared.

Egleston is a land of extremes. The silence can be ominous, the space airless, a memoriam to what might have been. Shouting was the counterpoint to silence, a clarion call for recognition. "Listen to me." "Look at me." The shouting was encouraged in part by a friendly competition, which established a pecking order. This lasted for one class. A clever teacher can take advantage of such competition by holding an "auction of excellence," bidding for answers and recognition in a warm way. I always thought that the shouting in class, like so much behavior at Egleston, was counterphobic, the outward expression of an inner cry. In some unwitting way, our kids were trying to compensate for years of neglect. We had too much yelling or too much silence. We had manic outbursts and paralyzing withdrawal, but little repose. These kids were trapped.

"The Heart"

Society's got a brother trapped . . .
some don't know how to act and others will stab you
in the back
And when you least expect it, yo' check it,
you'll end up with a jail record
for looking like the next kid
But it couldn't be me homie, NO NO
You might windup six-feet deep, homie,
'Cause burners burn, now turn and take a look

at a teen who's a fiend
snatching old ladies pocketbooks
No one helps, all he gets is a jail cell
Doing dead time, 'cause he can't make bail.
Now his nights are long and cold, straight up you gotta be bold
This is the truth, just a story untold
It's about the rough life my people got
a little kid on the block age nine shot
Word to God, I cried and I weeped
The anger is deep, at night I can't even sleep
I grab my gun, wishing that I never had this
Rolling with the badness now I'm caught up in the madness.

— *Demitri Robertson*

José, on his last day, exemplified a typical skewed logic in which geographical polar opposites, north and south, are used as if they are mutually exclusive.

I know Cuba and Russia are both communist countries, but what makes them friends? Cuba is much older than Russia, and they are close together. Cuba is south, and Russia is north, so why are they together? It's not so important where the missiles come from. This is a matter between us and Cuba.

By the time José disappeared from class, however, some of the kids in "First Person History" were thinking about the missile crisis as a global mind game, a matching of wits and nerve in which Kennedy and Khrushchev were trying to outwit each other. Jorge, Robert, and Marieca introduced us to psychohistory:

This thing doesn't depend on missiles. It depends on brains, who can see into the other's head. It's not even exactly brains. It's the kind of brains that psychologists have, you know, telling what somebody will do and why. The same kind of shit we have to do if some jerk threatens us.

How you know what's in anybody's head? How you goin' to write a psychology of history, of Khrushchev, when you don't even know what goes on in your own man's head? You do know some of what they did in the past, but does this mean they will do it again in the future? Maybe something different is on their mind.

This psychological stuff is hard to do, but I know from my life that my feelings make me do a lot of things I shouldn't. If you want to understand Kennedy and Khrushchev, to predict, isn't it better to concentrate on what they want from politics? I would look at what they want and see what's the best way for them to get it.

You smart, but you're also a dumb nigger. You got to use psychology to know if they got desires besides political. Maybe they crazy. Would somebody not crazy send missiles to Cuba when we got more than anybody?

Robert, Marieca, Kathy, and Jorge became more sophisticated and more skeptical. They began to think about actions and reactions they never would have considered two months earlier. They began to feel the counterpoint of the crisis. They criticized each other in serious ways and built on each other's arguments. "It depends on brains, who can see into the other's head." Jorge's comment was prophetic. Robert was thinking about Jorge's remarks about brains and strategy:

Niggers are never going to have brains, or I should say niggers are never going to develop their brains, get brainy, because the white man doesn't want him to think. That why keep the schools so bad they don't teach us the right stuff, and the AIDS, which they invented and then sent to the ghetto to kill us, to weaken us. And the dope, which they could stop if they wanted to. They don't because there's too much money in it—billions for the federal government and the cops, all the way up and down. Some cops here make more money from dealers than they do in the salary.

So if we can't develop our brain in the school, we have to do it in the streets. This school, our school, is different. Teachers care, and you can learn. But this school is used to show off, to let white people think they doing something. It's a show.

The kids in "First Person History" began to move to issues beyond the missile crisis. They were beginning to see connections between the Cold War and their own plight. It was clear that they were becoming politically conscious. Our exercise in the Cuban missile crisis was beginning to bear fruit:

Wait a minute. What does this whole thing cost? How many billions? If we put all that money in missiles, how much is going to be left for welfare and people like us? We going to lose our benefits.

Marieca amplified Shavon's economics.

From what I can see, most dudes in the army are black. So when we go to war, blacks die for white people. We be poor and can't get good jobs because we don't have skills. And we don't have skills because we black and Hispanic and poor and without daddies. So no one tells us school important. Mom's working all the time so don't have time. Everything be against us. It all fits together. The black army dying for whites, the poverty, the missing parent and poor, no one to push you. It's like Murray say, a system, a system, man, each part causes each part. Think, all that money could go to hospitals.

I tried to show Kathy, José, and the others that the schemes we used to study the missile crisis could be used to look at other historical problems—thinking about consequences, reducing uncertainty, anticipating unintended consequences, isolating causes and effects. I talked about how the theory of rational choice could be used to make more thoughtful decisions, not only in politics or economics but in daily life. We slowly calculated the comparative advantage of finishing high school and junior college and becoming a nurse in a safe environment as opposed to selling heroin, making a thousand dollars a day, and getting caught and convicted, and caught again, and exposed to the unpredictable behavior of addicts. Everyone understood rational choice when we assigned positive and negative values to all the variables, including peace of mind.

I appreciate the irony here: these were problem kids in alternative schools learning to think dialectically, kids being trained to perceive outcomes in beginnings, kids thinking out the power of ideology and the locus of power, always thinking about *why*. But the fact is that we did these things in "First Person History." We understood after some discussion the inverse relation of defense budgets and welfare. We began to appreciate the limits placed on the power of Kennedy and Khrushchev by their constituents. As we eliminated options that would be seriously opposed by allies, we came to realize that there is an international political system with complex animosities and alliances, that actions evoke reactions, and that the past always affects the present. We learned that classes have different degrees of control over the state. We learned that schools vary enormously between cities and suburbs and so do life chances:

"Who Am I?"

Today I feel like a bird flying high,
Yesterday I wished that I could die.
I dreamed I'm a seagull on the ocean's coast
Often I'm invisible, I have the soul of a ghost.

But who am I?
I work, I play, I cry, I laugh,
I try hard to succeed but see no path.
I'm young, I'm black, I'm out of reach
But I'm able to be taught, and able to teach.

But who am I?
In a hardship country is where I live,
Where everyone takes and no one gives.
Quite different am I from the people of this place
For I do not judge anyone by race.

But who am I?
I'm confused and ambivalent, I'm here and there,
I always end my day with a silent prayer.
        — Teressa Jones

I also decided to tackle the problem the kids had with ideas not obviously rooted in sensual reality. Events that were sequential or causal looked disconnected to the kids in class, as if events were isolated, unbonded, spontaneous and randomized bursts of energy:

What's Russia got to do with Cuba? Look, Russia tried its best. It sent these missiles thousands of miles to Cuba, and it probably cost a lot. But once they are in Cuba, Russia won't care what happens. They just want to shake up America. Russia and Cuba are different countries, thousands of miles apart. They are not connected and have nothing to do with one another.

I talked a bit about historiography and raised the issue of why their history turned out as it did. I repeated bits of the lecture I gave the first week I was at Egleston. I presented the theory that history is made by kings and queens. I spoke of Carlyle's theory that great men determine history and Plekhanov's theory that when circumstances require great men, they will be produced—that it is circumstances, not individuals, that create history. I talked about the power of ideology and presented the idea that history is the unfolding of God's plan. I spoke about Marx's materialist conception of history, the view that the labor process determines conflict and change. In every instance, I supplied examples because these kids have to pin down theory with concrete reality. So I gave three examples: Napoleon's role in creating a French empire, the way feudalism gave way to capitalism in Europe, and the impact of the absence of feudalism on American history. While I spoke, there was not a single word from the kids in "First Person History." No one left; there was no kidding around, just silence. The kids loved to play with big ideas that could not be immediately verified, but could in some way be related to their life:

Look at China. Makes America look small, iron and copper and coal. How many people you say live in China—a billion, two billion? And the Chinese are smart. Look at what they done. Chinese kids are smart. They say niggers are dumb. I heard Chinese don't care if they die.

Man, you crazy. Niggers are not dumb, no dumber than anyone else. And I'm sure that Chinese don't want to die more than anyone else. These are lies that cause wars and prejudice and all that shit. These lies are used by rich, power people to divide people so rich dudes can control them.

These were two high school dropouts who developed a theory about ideology and the use of stereotypes and prejudice. But the really beautiful moment was when Robert asked me how the universe began, and I told him what little I knew about the "big bang." He and Marieca asked the same questions that interest astrophysicists and philosophers. Robert asked, "How did the original ball of matter get there? Ain't no God, so who put it there, and why did it explode? What was there before the original matter? Do they know this? How fast is it expanding? Is there life in other places?"

Marieca was dumbfounded by the entire theory: "If the universe is slowing down, will it stop? What holds it together? Do they know what gravity is? I don't mean measuring it; I mean what it is made of." I think it was Kathy who asked, "If it's going out and slowing down, will it stop and then go in reverse to where it started?"

Egleston kids like to talk about the unexpected, the cataclysmic, the outer bounds of knowledge. Gradually I freed myself from any rigid plan and felt free to introduce anything at anytime that worked, anything that required us to think playfully—puzzles, games, case studies, current events, role-playing, debating. The kids had an enormous effect on me. I abandoned the rigid time table I followed for forty years in college because I realized that whatever they talked about was important to them and almost everything could be related to our main topic. Our class resembled a great river with dozens of tributaries. We developed an orderly disorder, much more suited to our needs than any formal and intimidating agenda. The kids became more spontaneous, and the class became more theirs than mine. I controlled the outer fringes of the talk.

I took advantage of our controlled chaos one day to experiment with a mind game I developed called the Deviant Case. I provided the class with the population figures for five countries and asked the students to speculate on the relation between populations and the countries' disposition to go to war. One country, India, did not support any of the theories they developed. It was the deviant case that forced them to reconsider and play with new variables.

One of the girls in class provided me with a perfect opening: "What is the distance between San Juan and Havana?" She was really asking me if Soviet missiles in Cuba endangered her relatives. Another question, "How big are Russia and the United States?" a question I had answered dozens of times. Wanetta was thinking about comparative advantage: "Do we have enough iron and copper and the stuff they make bombs out of to beat Russia?" The question provoked a cascade of answers, wrong answers, absurd answers. "You got nothing to worry about, Puerto Rico is thousands of miles away from Cuba. The missiles couldn't get there." "Nobody is interested in destroying Puerto Rico. There is nothing there except a bunch of Hispanics, and we know no one gives a shit about them. So don't worry."

When the laughter subsided, Gabriel, who sat in on occasion in the hope that I would mistake him for a regular and credit him for the course, estimated the populations of the United States and the former Soviet Union: "We are much bigger than Russia. It's too cold to live there. Maybe they got fifty million people maybe, a little more. America has twice as many—a hundred million. There must be fifty million Hispanics in America."

"Murray, when are minorities going to outnumber whites? I heard it's about eight years from now. Watch us move then. It will be a different game. Don't worry, we outnumber Russia."

"Look, we got nuclear bombs, and they got 'em, probably more because they got slave labor. So they got the natural resources, too. Neither one will fire. They both afraid of each other."

I asked if anyone had flown from Boston or New York to Puerto Rico and how long it took. "How fast do these planes go?"

Jorge, born in Cuba, replied authoritatively, "At least eighty miles per hour." "You crazy, man," Carlos replied, "they go at least two hundred miles. Everybody knows that."

"I flew to Puerto Rico from New York. It took about four hours. My boyfriend sent me there, my ex-husband. San Juan must be eight hundred miles from New York, two hundred times four." The discussion was surreal but typical.

The issue was distance, speed, and population. It was time to begin my game. I asked the class members if they knew the populations of China, Russia, Puerto Rico, India, and the United States. Again, wild guesses. "I know China the biggest—hundreds of millions, right, and Puerto Rico smallest, fifty million."

"Listen, sweetheart, I know Puerto Rico has just a few million, America a hundred million at least, and India's big, two hundred million." An atlas introduced us to reality.

I asked Gabriel to go to the blackboard because it forced this dreamy boy to pay attention. I always ask the most removed kids to answer questions or take notes for the class or act as discussion leader because shock therapy sometimes works. Demand in the school on occasion stimulates supply. I told Jorge that he was a famous military historian from Mars who had these facts and nothing more and that he was ordered by the Martian High Command to report on the military potential of these five nations. Jorge responded immediately, stood tall, a distinguished military historian, erect bearing, slow, pompous speech. Role-playing had that effect on Egleston kids, even the most removed.

Our Martian military historian was bewildered at first: "I don't see the point, but is it that the population of a country makes its military— big country and lot of people, big army?"

"Why?"

"I don't know."

"Yes, you do. Think, damn it, think. Don't let us down. Take your time. How does manpower relate to power? Manpower and strength. What can you do with a large population that you can't do with a small population? Jorge, you do know."

"Is it that the more people you have, the more you can replace the dead soldiers? A big country like China have any amount of replacements. Puerto Rico can't do this. Cuba can't do this."

"Good, good, nice thinking. Give me another advantage of large populations. Do you know that most soldiers work supplying fighting soldiers? Do you get the point?"

"No, I don't."

"Yes, you do. The men behind the soldiers, supplying."

"I don't know."

"Yes, you do. Do armies need uniforms, guns, shoes, tanks?"

"Oh, you mean the people in factories?"

"Yes, yes, yes."

"The big countries will be able to build more factories and make more uniforms because they have more people, and therefore they can have more of everything. It all fits together—more supplying, more fighting, more dying, more to replace the dead with. Look what we study: America with plenty of population and Russia. It's population that causes wars, no, that makes war possible." Jorge was beginning to smile and feel proud.

"Is there anything else that's important that might make a country warlike?"

Jorge, flushed from his previous triumph, did not hesitate. Small successes breed triumphs at Egleston. "Got to have the stuff you make the nuclear bombs out of, and you got to have iron and steel—you know, minerals for war—so when I write my report to Mars, I will have my assistants check minerals. I'll have them do a map of where the minerals are and map of the population."

Miriam, another girl with a history (twenty-two, viciously abused by her husband, escaped, divorced, mother of a two-year-old, one of our brightest girls who had been preparing for the S.A.T. in another class with me), could move beyond the point where others became exhausted. She picked up on Jorge's map. "Don't you see that if you put one map on top of the other, you can really see who can practice war? When population and minerals overlap, there is power."

"What can we learn from the history of these five countries?" Our man from Mars was silent. Wanneta, a tiny but bombastic girl, a fusion of the Delphic oracle and Walter Winchell, could not tolerate Jorge's hesitancy.

The history of a country be like the history of a person. It has its ups and down, patterns, certain ways of behaving. If a person tries to settle them, you can bet that person won't go to war very often, and I suppose it's true of nations. They all have a rhythm, people and nations. So the past, history, I like that, it comes from *his story*, tells a lot about what the future be. So, Mars man, you got your story, population, resources, history.

Miriam was raising her hand and stamping her foot impatiently. "I have a bigger idea which explains more. It's not just that they can supply more or have more natural resources. There is another reason for them to be warlike: they know they can make war, so there is more chance they will."
"Miriam, is there a rule here?"

Yeah, If you can, you probably will. So you can see what's going to happen from the past and from population and resources. If a country like China has a big population, China will have to feed them, and China will probably invade other countries to get food and iron and coal. So what a country needs will determine what it does about war.

"Miriam, that was terrific. Much history is just about what you say. You're terrific."
Miriam wasn't finished:

There's more. In a country like China, the number of people is so big that everybody must feel powerful, feel big. It's just like a big gang. They will feel more aggressive and be more aggressive with so many people. And dying won't be as important as here. War may even be a way to get respect and honor.

Shavon extended Miriam's remarks:

So making war and losing millions won't be so big. It won't be a question of life and death. The big countries will beat up on the small ones. The U.S. will eat Puerto Rico, and Russia will eat all the countries around it. I don't know their names. It's like us, the hood, Dorchester, Jamaica Plain, Roxbury, the big gangs beat on the little. And the more powerful swallow the little.

It was now time to introduce the deviant case:

Your theories about population and war are good, but India has a very large population, 850 million, and a modest army. They have had wars with their neighbor, Pakistan, and skirmishes with China; but India decided not to be a major military power. A very large population but not basically warlike, it doesn't fit your theory. There is also Germany, not on our list, but a country with an average population for Europe and yet an aggressive, warlike country. Soldiering is an honored profession there. So how would you deal with India, and maybe later, Germany?

Shavon, always drawing on her own experience, suggested, "Is it one has not been disrespected and other has? I bet somebody beat one of them in a big war, really beat 'em, really dissed 'em, and they going to get even. Countries, people, all the same, all beat on, all want revenge. Murray, that's the way it is."

"Yes, Germany was beaten in 1918 and dissed. Countries sometimes go to war when their national honor has been soiled."

Miriam was unimpressed. She kept shaking her head, impatient with Shavon and me: "Got to be something special in India, something different.

Something that gets most Indians. Is that what you call them? Is it religion? Is it their idea about right and wrong, about killing and violence? Something big."

"Are you telling us that India has not been a major military force because of its religion?"

"I don't know. Maybe. Maybe religion can be a big thing, look at the Christians—and people do live by ideas of right and wrong."

"You're right. Ideas can be very important, but what ideas would make India pacific?"

"Make India what? Pacific, what does it mean?"

"You know the Pacific Ocean?" Complete silence. "What is a pacifier?"

"Makes a kid quiet."

"Yes, quiet, but peaceful is better. So what ideas might make India relatively peaceful?"

Jorge shouted, "Ideas about war and violence."

"Who did Martin Luther King learn from?"

"That Indian guy, what's his name?"

"Gandhi. What did King believe in?"

"Peace."

"But what strategy, what tactic did he follow?"

"Peace, peace."

"What is nonviolence?"

"It's letting the other guy hit you and you don't hit back. It's stupid. You be killed."

I asked Shavon to imagine how the police or the army look on television when the victims refuse to fight back.

"I see, I see. They look like killers, like they do something wrong. They look bad. I saw the police firehose kids in the South on television. They look like killers. Ask me how the kids looked."

"How?"

"Like victims."

"So what about right and wrong, what about the morality and justice of the cops and the kids?"

Miriam immediately saw the point: "Nonviolence make it simple—who is moral and who isn't."

"And what does nonviolence do to the victims?"

No one responded. I always let the silence build up until the kids felt uncomfortable. The tension often forced a response.

"It makes the victims be one, feel one. It unites them, makes them stronger with morals." "You're right."

Everyone screamed—a lot of high fives while Shavon accepted congratulations and bowed to her audience.

"So why might India not be so warlike?" Miriam understood: "Doesn't it make everything clearer? The cops look exactly what they are, bullies and crooks. And the poor or the protestors be like what they are, poor, weak, powerless. But they also look together, like one and right. It gets clearer that's what nonviolence does."

Miriam turned to India: "Gandhi's ideas and his memory must be very important in India today. Like a religion. So ideas can be very important. Maybe more important than natural resources and population because ideas control what's in peoples' minds. But how do you measure these things?"

I found the smallness of the class to be a critical condition for learning. Kids were embarrassed when they didn't meet our standards, so evident in this small setting, and very pleased when they did. The tiny setting magnified everything. Kennedy's words and Khrushchev's pronouncements became vibrant, inescapable reminders of the holocaust that might have been. Role-playing gave us a tough McNamara and a thunderous Khrushchev. For one hour on Thursdays, we felt we were in a special place, Kennedy's office, and it was McNamara and Rusk speaking, not Marieca or Robert.

Our little theater became lifelike when the kids in "First Person History" came to hate Rusk: "Rusk is an asshole. Who cares about Berlin? It's thousands of miles away and no mind. We got to find a way to negotiate with Khrushchev. We got to give him something. People won't negotiate unless they get something. We have to let him not look like an asshole."

Robert, Marieca, and Jorge remembered more of our previous weeks' work as they became more involved. This improvement permitted us to deal in more sophisticated ways with the crisis. Marieca, for example, became perplexed by the worldwide propaganda war conducted by Kennedy and Khrushchev. She began to appreciate Khrushchev's wariness of America:

Is Khrushchev telling the truth? Did American soldiers go to Russia? You can see why Russia is worried about America and hates America, missile bases in Turkey. Russia must be scared shitless.

Robert extended Marieca's insight:

He must want those missiles out of there. Maybe he put the missiles in Cuba to bargain. But it is also about Berlin. Remember, we read that memo to Kennedy about Russia invading Berlin. There are a lot of reasons why Russia sent the missiles, a lot of bargains they can make. And they are right about the blockade of Cuba, violates the law of oceans. This dude has a lot going for him—and what about us flying planes over Cuba illegally? I predict he won't back down.

They became interested in the question of how Kennedy could make a rational choice when so much information was missing or false. I showed the class how one could infer from partial information—that we could infer the power and range of missiles from their size, and the number of missiles from the number of Russian workers in Cuba. Marieca reminded us that someone in the Oval Office said we had photographs of Russian missiles in the May Day parade, and she proposed that we could compare these photographs with those of Cuban missiles. Jorge suggested:

Turkish missiles threatening Russia, this guy believes he is not the aggressor, that he is legal and that he won't back down without getting something big out of this. How about this? He sent Russians to Cuba to fire the missiles. He's not fooling. That's why he sent Russian soldiers. They know how to operate these things. If he let Cubans run the missiles, you know it's a joke. You can tell from what people did in the past what they will do.

"First Person History," as I noted before, succeeded and failed. I could not involve some of the students. They missed at least a third of our classes. One of them was high on occasion. The missile crisis was a minor excursion for them; none of them took school seriously. None of them seemed to believe that Egleston could prepare them for some reasonable future. They were bored. They were polite. They were silent.

I did everything I could. I called on them more frequently. I praised them whenever they gave even the most partial answer. I reaffirmed them at every possible moment. I offered to tutor them after class—all to no avail. We made dates. They failed to appear. Most of the time they said "I don't know" or gave answers that were simply repetitions of the question heightened by an affirmative tone. Sometimes they made a wild guess that utilized a fact or phrase out of context: "Douglas, why did Khrushchev argue so strongly that the American blockade was illegal?"

"Because the American blockade was illegal."

"But why did he keep repeating this?"

"Because it is illegal."

His "answer" is without context. He sees no purpose in Khrushchev's insistence. Douglas does not understand that Khrushchev wanted to delegitimate America's actions. I asked Kathy why Khrushchev placed missiles in Cuba. "Because he wanted to. They was together because there was already some missiles in Cuba."

On November 1, the day of our eighth meeting, only Kathy appeared. Six people, including a young boy, had been shot in a gang war between two housing projects. Douglas and Robert lived in one of these projects and were with the families of the young boy, who died the next day. Cynthia was absent per usual, and I hadn't seen William for two weeks. This is not unusual for Egleston. The previous year Angela had disappeared for four weeks, returned, and told her teachers she had been in Florida visiting her grandmother. Nothing happened. She lost no points. She was not reprimanded. No one checked her story. Marieca disappeared when the term ended. She had been missing for weeks. I asked, "Where is Marieca?" People shrugged their shoulders and said, "We can't deal with her." "She is out of control." "Marieca will return." Very few questions were asked. Patricia, the principal, always said, "this is an alternative school," and the teachers reminded me that we have the kids who can't deal with regular high school:

Murray, our kids have no patience. They cannot concentrate. They can't stay with a project. They have behavior problems. Many are involved in substance abuse. Our attendance is 47 percent. The minds of these kids are not in school. We have ten or twelve girls with children. Yes, we need more discipline. We need to see that kids are in class and on time. But you know our kids suffer abuse of all kinds, poverty, one-parent families, violence, drugs, no jobs. The discipline can only do so much. Yes, we have to remain in charge, make the kids work, keep deadlines, go to class. But, and this is a big but, our kids need self-esteem. They are fragile. They need plenty of praise even for little things. So we travel a difficult road—discipline, the possibility of failure, loss of self-esteem.

But Murray, these kids are going to live in the real world. They must get to work on time, and work, and meet deadlines, so, for me, the discipline is very important.

"Kathy, do you know where Russia is?"
"No."
"How far is Cuba from the U.S.?"
"Two thousand miles from Miami."
I corrected Kathy.
"So the missiles from Cuba will get to the U.S. faster than from Russia because Cuba is so close."
"What can they negotiate about?"
"About the war."
"What will the U.S. get from negotiations?"
"Not having a war?"
"And what will Russia get out of this?"
"I don't know. No war. Russia will get their missiles back. I don't know. Russia's a little country, much smaller than the United States, and they must have only a few missiles."
"Did you ever hear us talk about American missiles in Turkey?"
"No."
Weeks before Kathy had talked intelligently about mutual deterrence, and she argued the case for negotiation. Now she claimed ignorance. This is a common occurrence for Egleston students—a week of disassociation, a week of reality, remembrance of things past followed by amnesia.

When I explained that we had missiles in Turkey and that Turkey bordered Russia, facts that we had noted dozens of times, Kathy understood: "The missiles would be quicker to get there if Russia bombed us. So you take your missiles from Turkey and you take your missiles from Cuba."

"Do you see a reason here why Khrushchev sent the missiles to Cuba?"

"Sure, so he can force us to exchange, Cuba, Turkey, missile for missile. He is very smart to find a way to get rid of missiles in Turkey without war."

"Kathy, if you were Kennedy, what information would you want?" Without hesitation, Kathy responded, speaking quickly, which is not her style, as if she were the premier historian of the crisis: "How many are there? Where are they? Where are they pointed? What kind is it? What can it do? How powerful it is?"

"What would you like to know about Khrushchev?"

"What he is thinking about. What he wants to get out of this. Will he shoot nuclear if he doesn't get what he wants? Will he negotiate? I learned from you, I remember, that Kennedy and Khrushchev have to satisfy politics and army at home. How stubborn is he?"

A lot of Egleston kids are sharp. As I have said before, the problem here is not brain power but nihilism and self-hatred, the twin scourges of the hood. And this is why the inner-city high school often fails. The school liberates some kids, but by itself it can never reconstruct the culture and the political economy of the ghetto, which makes Kathy and Jorge what they are. Europe and Asia do not exist for them. The legacy of Greece and Rome is unheard of. There is no Protestant Reformation, no Enlightenment, and no liberal tradition in America. American history begins about three weeks ago. Our Latino students know they are from Colombia or Guatemala, but they know nothing about their origins. Our black students know that their ancestors came from Africa and were sold into slavery, but they know little else.

During good days, when the kids in "First Person History" were enjoying the work, I used to fantasize that our little tutorial would have ripple effects that would change someone's life in ways we would never know. This fantasy was one of the props I used to steel myself against the days when Robert was absent and Marieca was drunk and Jorge was high, and Kathy was so furious at her abusive mother that she could barely talk in class. My vision of a great chain of learning, of black and Latino communities nourished by mutual aid, forged in small part by the kids we taught, was one of the dreams that kept me going.

This dream was shattered and restored almost every week. Egleston could be exhilarating. Students would meet every class for weeks, do most of the homework, respond in class, and my mind would fill with tears of hope. And then they would disappear. I felt a bond with Kathy and Marieca and Robert, a fellowship based on beating the odds, beating the ghetto, beating the alcohol and the dope, the violence and the abuse.

My private vision did not seem absurd when a student who had been mute suddenly asked an amazing question: "What was the effect on Khrushchev's popularity in Russia of sending missiles to Cuba? Did the army go with him? Did he think he could gain from this, and what?" Egleston could be exhilarating. Robert would not drop the subject of canals after I had spent an hour on geography. "How do they get the water to rise and fall? How do they make engines big enough to move the locks? Can you get a battleship through?"

Marieca asked me:

How do you get all of these ideas by reading just a number or a few words? You see things in this report I don't see. Teach me how. My teachers didn't ask me questions like, "If you've got one thing and another thing and another, what does it mean?" Nobody taught us to relate all those things and make sense out of them. You keep talking about what's the cause, what's the effect, what's the context, what's the consequences? I want to know how to do all these things. I never thought about this, worrying about our allies and world public opinion. How you know all this? All I ever did in school was repeat what I read. Tell me.

I felt like embracing Marieca. I told her we would learn together. A week after Marieca asked for help, she dreamed that she was Kennedy confronted with the missile crisis:

I'm embarrassed to tell you this. I feel funny about it. But last night I dreamed that I was Kennedy in the middle of the missile crisis. I was sitting there wondering whether I should invade or bomb Cuba or just the missiles, or appeal to the U.N., or boycott Cuba, or threaten Russia to get back at them. I couldn't decide, and I was frightened and upset. I just couldn't decide, and everybody kept giving me advice—yes, no, maybe. It was terrible. And I woke up in a sweat. Thank God I woke up!

❧

"This Is About Using Racism for Politics": God, TV, and Politicians

Believing in things does not make them real. Tell yourself you are rich, and go and buy a Cadillac. Do you think you'll get it? What's real is real, no matter what you believe. Tell yourself you will get a perfect mark on the SAT, and then take it. The same is true for Martin Luther King. Blacks believed in his power, his words, and they believed that he would lead to black freedom. And they are wrong. Look at where we live. Look at Roxbury. History is made by money, the big money. The big companies, Ford, buy the government. They get what they want.

Many kids at Egleston think that teachers underestimate them. During my years at the school, I decided to overestimate them. I thought about what excited my students forty years ago at Columbia College when I taught Contemporary Civilization, a history of social thought from Plato to yesterday. I thought of Freud's treatment of aggression in *Civilization and Its Discontents*, or Hobbes's theory of the war of all against all, trenchant issues for the ghetto. And then I would look at the class, and my heart would sink: one kid adjusting his beeper, another dozing, one reading the paper, the rest motionless, a mournful negation of life.

At these moments, I would introduce something way out that might touch some deep conviction or fear. The first time I brought up God and history was during a lecture I gave to introduce myself to the students and teachers, a lecture which provoked much controversy. The discussion had gone like this:

God has my vote. Only a god knows enough to make something as big as history, to make so many people. Who made flowers and the sun? Sure, it's not man. Man don't make history. If he did, he wouldn't kill so much and war on people.

Bullshit, you swallow all that church shit. If God makes history, why are we niggers here living like shit? If God makes things, he a terrible god—so much disease and pain and poverty and killing, and don't tell me we don't know his secret purpose. We suffer for a better life we don't know about. That's shit, too. History is just like the ghetto, or the cocaine trade, or the government. Everything's run by the big guys, not one-great-man theory, but five, ten, twenty great men determine history. And they all do business with each other and protect each other. And they get very rich, very rich. And they make history all over the world, not just in one country. I suppose you could say that a conspiracy of great men runs things, and they fuck us every day. And let me tell you that this idea of inventions making history and workers winning is also a lot of shit. Tell me where have workers won?

You're all wrong. History is made by great men, not just rich big crooks, by great men made by bad circumstances. Look at Martin or Malcolm. Why did Malcolm rise and say those things? Because black people be ready for his words. They was beginning to get smart, and they knew white men fucked them. And they had some money taken together so they be ready for Malcolm, so a Malcolm came—same with Martin—South ready to listen, fed up with bein' niggers.

I was goin' with a dude who started to treat me bad, so I said, you are somebody, not a bitch. You go to school and learn and do well, you know things, you going to be someone, so I said goodbye. Never saw him again. So my theory of history is that each person makes his own history.

The kids in "First Person History" learned to speculate and on occasion to support their theories with facts from their life or some moral or religious scheme. In simple ways, they advanced theories of history that have been prominent for centuries: God as historical creator, a godless Darwinian struggle, history as conspiracy, history as oligarchy, history as a parade of pregnant circumstances producing great men, personal history as accumulated wisdom. Robert even advanced the idea that a proletarian revolution would fail.

Everyone was excited. Theories and counter-theories—an awakening, something truly marvelous, grand historiography, energizing the imagination of kids who had never thought about what makes history. It was not the mere speculation that pleased me; it was the ability of these students to develop counter-arguments.

During the next semester of "First Person History," I again raised the issue of whether God or the economy or great men or the big corporations or the Medellín cartel make history. If God made history, I asked, why are you kids in such bad shape?

God has nothing to do with history. And if he did, would Black people be here? God doesn't exist. This God business is bullshit. God was invented by people cause they are scared, afraid of the world, a lonely place. People be alone. They want comfort so they invent this dude. People be afraid of dying so they invent ideas that say they live forever. God was invented by rich people to keep poor people down.

Shavon's ideas were too simplistic for Wanneta:

God has a lot to do with history, and many believe in him. Even if there is no God, believing in him makes him real. Same true for ideas. They don't have to be real, only believed in.

Miriam concurred:

If people believe in an idea, even if it isn't so, it will make them do things. Look at sin. So they confess or worry or think they go to hell. This is real. Believe it, it's real. It makes people behave.

The kids who took "First Person History" for a second time were beginning to think more deeply. With no training, they not only developed some of the important ideas advanced by Hegel and Feuerbach, Berkeley and Marx, but even critiqued them with arguments fashionable in the eighteenth century.

I tried to bring the discussion home. I asked the kids what they did to feel more secure when they were frightened. "My grandmother believes that certain sacrifices will bring her good luck and long life, so she does them. If she believes it, it may be true for her."

"Maybe," Miriam said, introducing a sophisticated note, "but that doesn't mean it's true for other people. And what if she has bad luck, will she still sacrifice?"

"No, she'll just say, she always says, it's God's will." The kids in "First Person History" often used their discussion of God and history to expose some deep feelings and unresolved personal issues. Our class was often autobiographical, although I don't think the kids realized that they were talking about their own fate, their anger, their life, when they talked about God's will and God's power.

For these kids, even God is an agent of sinister forces, a tool of the rich, who sealed the fate of the blacks and caused them to suffer:

Wanneta is right about the rich make God, to get the poor, like us, to accept where we be because God make us to be poor. God made the suffering. God make the black people suffer, so it must be O.K. It's a great idea if you white and rich. Keep your place, nigger.

Robert compared life to a play in which the actors, who have no free will, must follow the script:

None of you dudes talk about what can happen and what we got no control over, what has to happen. Don't you think some of us will get killed? Everyone in this room lost someone. Things are set up so some of us be killed. It's like a play, everyone is set up in advance. I think this is what Murray calls necessity, right? Where Murray lives, a different play—money, suburbs, high school, college, be a doctor or a lawyer, no one get shot, like it's in the cards.

I know how people work is important. Look at the teachers here, and look at the people in the projects. Their work and their education makes them different. Your work takes a lot of the day and what you do, brain work or garbage work, makes people think one way and act one way, and, I guess, it makes their personality. But does work make history? No. Money makes history. They got the power, they pay for elections; they control politicians and get what they want. They make history. Your work may make you.

This was an amazing discussion for high school kids. Shavon, Miriam, Robert, and Wanneta touched upon some classics of political theory, and they did so with finesse. They were not in command of the details or refinements of these theories, but they understood the core.

They believed that the economy plays a major role in shaping history. They assumed that human nature can be changed by employment. These kids talked of power and powerlessness. They knew it's better to own labor power than to sell it. They were shrewd enough to believe that the rich use God to regulate the poor. They had some idea of the role of ideology. They realized that American ideas train them to be loyal. They were painfully aware of necessity—a kind of economic predestination. They even used the idea that reality is theater, a play in which the actors' roles are written long before the play opens. There is a richness here, an untapped reservoir of myth, prejudice, imagination, and insight.

But there is also the fantastic but understandable conspiracy that Shavon sees, a version of Robert's, which is that the United States government developed the AIDS virus and distributed it to the ghetto to eliminate minorities. This apocolyptic version of the paranoid style in American politics complements Shavon's claim that drugs determine history and pacify black soldiers:

We never talk about the real theory: the drug theory. Drugs make history. There's drugs everywhere, particularly in government. They control it, and they use it to keep some people rich and to put down minorities. There would be unemployment without it. I don't believe more money is spent on cars or food than drugs.

There is another theory of history. All the money drugs make can be used for guns and the army, and that's the connection between drugs and what a country need to be powerful. White people don't know. Think of all the drugs used in the army. Do you think these guys would fight if they weren't on drugs? Now, Murray, you know that you got to be crazy to fight in the army, crazy for a nigger. So the drugs is part of what the white man uses to put minorities down.

Shavon believes, as conspiratorial theorists generally do, that no one really understands the truth except the government. Whatever the truth may be, it is sinister, portentous, a well-guarded secret. The state has vast and irresponsible power, which it uses to magnify itself and diminish the power of the poor and minorities. The visible fact in the ghetto that successful dealers make a lot of money lends credence to the central idea that the government, an infinitely more powerful player than drug dealers, must make untold fortunes.

Shavon's theory implies that the purpose of the democratic state has been perverted, that America is now a drug-financed oligarchy that uses drugs (Robert would say AIDS) as a technique of social control. The theory may be absurd, but it is important to understand why intelligent kids like Robert and Shavon construct these edifices: the raw materials are present and plentiful, lots of drugs, many dying of AIDS. And the state can apparently not prevent either. The area is poor. Life is danger-ous. The contrast with the rest of America as magnified on television is enormous. It is easy for them to conclude that only a vast and powerful conspiracy could have caused this desolation.

In Egleston Square there is only the present. Egleston kids deal with this bleak image by lapsing into fantasies of grandiose careers as doctors or lawyers. The fantasy career is part of a larger psychological pose. Except for those who are visibly and painfully depressed, the student body is full of life, exuberant, full of fun and talk. Many girls bring their babies to school; mothers are affectionate and attentive. There is a lot of gossip, a lot of talk about boyfriends and about sports, very little talk about school, and literally no talk about future plans, a denial that helps maintain some emotional equilibrium. Years ago I audited a graduate seminar in political sociology in which the professor, a famous Marxist scholar and a refugee from Hitler, asked us to analyze television "soaps" and ads for several days. The experience was fascinating. During my third year at Egleston, I decided to do the same with the kids who took my class (remember that I was teaching high school dropouts as if they were graduate students). After all, these were kids who loved television and watched seven or eight hours a day, seduced by the tube as if it were a breast from which they sucked some life-giving milk:

Yeah, I watch many hours every day. I love my programs. They let me forget all the shit at home and on the street. And sometimes I think I am a beautiful white model. I get lost with all the soap operas, become the good girlfriend or the bad wife. I learn white ways, and I learn how wicked they are.

I watch TV because it excites me, mostly movies, *Rambo*, Steven Seagal, *Terminator*. These guys know how to do it, how to blast their enemies, bang, bang, how to get exactly what they want, not afraid to shoot or kill, not afraid to die. They could teach us plenty. You've got to *take*. No one will give. Got to be ready to grab it.

Nobody believes me, but I like the ads, sometimes better than the programs. The ads is beautiful, and they show me all the wonderful things I could have if I was rich, which I ain't. I be poor, but I can dream.

Their looking and imagining interested me. If television excited these students, why not use it as a prime source? Why not treat soap operas and advertisements seriously, as if they were literature? There was much that could be learned by thoughtful watching. Is the Cosby show about a black or white family? Why is the late-evening news entertainment and not news? What is news? How do Estée Lauder and Revlon and Calvin Klein seduce viewers? Are they really selling love or perfume?

I asked our class to watch television for three or four nights and keep a record of these questions. I suggested that they look particularly for the hidden and unspoken benefits that advertisers use to entice viewers. I introduced them to a famous Revlon ad in which a dramatically beautiful and bosomy girl runs down a verdant meadow, in sweater and pearls, breasts bouncing, hair perfectly in place, teeth gleaming, to embrace a handsome, beautifully groomed, perfectly tailored male model who embraces her tenderly and coos, "I love you." She responds, "It's Revlon."

"What's going on?" I asked. No one spoke. Then everyone burst out laughing, because (unlike most whites) they saw the ad as surreal, a theater of the absurd, the kind of romantic masturbation that whites can relate to but that looks totally phony to blacks who don't hang out in meadows, don't wear cashmere sweaters and pearls, and don't embrace handsome white models in double-breasted blue blazers.

Wanneta made the commentary:

White people are dumb if they fall in love with a smell, really dumb. But it's more. If you wear Revlon guys will fall in love with you. Wear Revlon, and you'll get love. Use Revlon, and you'll find love. No black man would be that stupid. They might go for sex or money or because the two like each other, but never for a smell. This would only work for white people who can be suckered. Smell good, get love. This is white shit.

Again more laughter, which made me realize that these kids are strengthened by their distance from white reality, an estrangement that permits them to note instinctively the madness of so much that impresses whites. Black pride, which is important to some Egleston kids, is strengthened by their perception of the white world as an asylum.

Despite this view, Egleston kids are becoming "white." They consume to the extent their pocketbooks allow, and they ape white teenagers. They are unable to keep pace, however, because whiteness is too expensive for them. So I asked them during our little television orgy to think about what the white world offers them on the tube. Robert extended Wanneta's remarks in that special tone of his, diffident yet authoritative, as if he were talking to children. He always began with "You gotta realize," as if no one in the room ever did:

It's not just perfume. It's everything. They are telling us that if you buy their stuff or their cigarettes or cars, you get something big in addition to smoking and driving. The cigarette makes you look smooth, macho, a big man. And the big car, the pimp car. Isn't it obvious, a big man, a big car, a rich man, and the Revlon smell will get your love? So you have to look out, man, nothing looks like what it looks like. Man's got to get behind these ads to see what's up. You got to find the benefit behind the cigarette, and I suppose Murray is going to teach us to look behind because, shit, if we can't do that, they will always get us.

The discovery of coded messages and symbolic manipulation in television advertising was the kind of insight that gave weight to conspiratorial theories. Robert was convinced that unless he learned how to look behind the advertisements "they will always get us." He assumed that there is a malevolent white world, racist, conspiratorial, powerful, ready to plunder black men. White men might be stupid and crazy, they may confuse love and smells, but they were hardheaded about seducing black people and conspiring to sell cigarettes and cars.

Robert tried to convince the class members that their welfare was profoundly altered by these merchant conspirators. The class was beginning to feel uncomfortable, duped by the very television ads the students had enjoyed. For them, like so many adolescents, ads fuse with the program, another colorful spectacle verified by Michael and Shack. But Robert was telling them to be wary, and Shavon was getting angry at the thought of being victimized:

These ads disrespect us, disrespect our intelligence, make us look stupid, get us to buy what we really don't want. Isn't it part of that white thing, that conspiracy to make us poor and weak? I remember a long time ago, when Murray was talking about the big billboard ad for cigarettes in Egleston Square and how surprised I was when he pointed out that there were no billboards like that in Newton—suburbs wouldn't let it in. All these doctors and lawyers got money, and they know what to do in politics. People listen to them. No one listens to us. They don't want smoking. So we weak, can't stop cigarette ads, so we can be affected.

Three years earlier, Shavon had been in a state of suspended animation, battered by fear of the police, crazed addicts, and long, cold nights. She now talked in class incessantly. She wanted to be respected yet felt comfortable enough to present strong and thoughtful views. She had learned that conflict was a useful way of looking at society, and she tried to think systemically. She was smart enough to realize that there was much to be learned by comparing Egleston Square with an affluent suburb. She was very much aware of power and powerlessness and understood why towns like Newton could prevent cigarette ads and Egleston could not.

But Shavon still missed classes and lost interest easily. She had trouble sitting still. She knew that a community college might open some careers to her, but she also knew that jobs were scarce and her skills few. She often told me she was tired and weary, too hassled to study. She was now pregnant.

During the winter of our third year together, I noticed that Wanneta and Shavon were carrying books and pamphlets on Rastafarianism, the religion to which they were now devoted. They were full of missionary zeal and insisted that we suspend our work temporarily and give some time to their new religion. I asked them to talk to us the following week about why they were attracted to Rastafarianism and to prepare an outline of the main ideas so we could follow more easily. I was reluctant to allow this interruption because the class was just developing a feel for the dynamics of advertising, but Wanneta and Shavon were so enthusiastic about these ideas that I thought it was good for them to get a hearing.

The two failed to appear in the following two weeks. They never wrote anything for us. They never raised the subject again. I don't know if they were frightened by the thought of going public with their new religion or just irresponsible. I was surprised, disappointed actually.

By our third year, the kids had become accustomed to our method. They looked for wider meanings, latent functions, coded messages, causes and effects. And they were beginning to think about systems. Television ads gave us an opportunity to use our method because TV was the drug of choice for many kids. They had seen thousands of ads and now had a chance to watch seriously and decipher some of Madison Avenue's coded messages. Television can be a great teacher: it doesn't look or feel like school work, but it can be a rich resource for teaching—melodrama, history, science, tragedy, greed, heroism, violence—all are there to be exploited by teachers who help students see the ways in which art imitates life.

As if she were on cue, Wanneta asked, "Give us another ad so we can look behind." So I used my favorite from graduate school, an ad that promised almost all the fruits of bourgeois life: sex, power, money, and status. I described the ad. Many years ago Chrysler employed Ricardo Montalban, a handsome Latin romantic lead, to advertise a luxury car, the Chrysler Cordoba convertible. Like all good ads, this was theater. The ad opens with Montalban leaning on the hood of a beautiful black convertible, which he is gently stroking. He talks; he strokes. A magnificent mansion and beautiful gardens form the background. Montalban strokes the hood again and says something like, "You can really ride this car like a man, smooth, big, powerful, fast. This is a man's car. Look at the beautiful instrument panel, easy to turn on and off. The soft leather seats." Montalban then strokes the leather seat, sits down in the driver's seat, and says, "Smooth, beautiful, rich." He then sits in the rear seat and says, "You can really mount this seat, a perfect fit."

Everyone burst out laughing. Rita, who dropped in from time to time, thought the ad was vulgar. Others thought it epitomized the craziness of white men:

This is ridiculous. First of all, I don't see anything hidden here. It's an ad for a car, that's it. We laugh because it's all so phony, house, car, man. It has nothing to do with us. We can't afford any of that shit. It is unreal. Makes the white man look money mad. No, that's not right. Makes him look like a stick, a cartoon character, not real, no life. This stick is in love with a car. He loves a car. The car is his woman. That's sick. One guy falls in love with perfume, the other guy with a car. And you are going to tell me we should become part of this crazy shit? Murray, you're losing your cool.

Kanil was trying to say that the white world was mad, abstracted, and sexless. He intimated that for all the problems Egleston kids had, they were still alive and sexual.

This guy in the ad, he doesn't look to me as if he could shake it. Everything in the ad is sort of dead—too perfect, no life. You know white man can't dance, can't rap, can't play. We can feel. We can cry. We can love. We can be grieving. We are alive.

We were at a critical moment. The kids at Egleston woefully lack self-esteem. But Kanil was reaffirming black energy, relishing a life force that he felt was uniquely black. He was telling the class to feel good about themselves, and it was this ridiculous ad for white men that did it.

Wanneta capped the conversation, shivering as she spoke as people do when they think of rats or snakes: "I could never sleep with a white man." Her remark had a surrealist quality for me, as if it were spoken in *Star Trek* by aliens who felt so superior to Captain Kirk and his colleagues that sexual contact with them was utterly repulsive.

I asked, "What is this ad all about? Remember, the Revlon ad, bits were symbolic. The perfume was not just a smell. It was a love potion. In these ads, things stand for other things and the ad promises a big payoff. What about the Chrysler? Is it just a car? What about those soft leather seats you ride in?" Rita, who dropped in on occasion as if the class were a health spa she went to for group support to lose a few pounds, reassured everyone, "There ain't no secret here. Just rich, white folks playing with toys, an expensive car, an expensive house, selling cars, nothing weird. I don't see any of the secrets you are talking about." Alourdes, like most Egleston kids, was literal minded. For her, a car was a car. There were no psychological nuances or double meanings, no shades of color, just black and white. There were no secret languages, no metaphors, no symbolic content. This pristine empiricism dominated Egleston thinking—for good reasons, I think. It made life in dangerous circumstances seem more secure. The world had to be just as it appeared to be, concrete and predictable, in order to move safely.

For three years, our work was designed, among other things, to coax these kids away from their empiricism and help them learn how to think abstractly. Almost every conversation in class began with simple reca-pitulations or repetition. "Why," I asked, "is a handsome man leaning on the hood of this car?"

Wanneta winked. "He is tired."

Everyone laughed. The more political kids and the very angry ones are forced to abandon this simple empiricism because they want some explanation of their powerlessness, and they can find this only if they make some connections between the rich and the poor or between the state and the drug trade and develop some theory. Conspiratorial theory is their most common resource. The conspirators are the local cops, white politicians, Washington, school teachers, and the rich. The students believe they are victimized by a smart and avaricious white world that uses them to fight wars and then clean urinals. Shavon exemplified this school of thought:

Didn't we see a secret message in that Revlon ad? Haven't we learned that white men take advantage of us whenever they can, with secret, hidden things, things we cannot understand? So we know things ain't what they look like—always something secret, something behind, something sneaky that makes them rich, and something that gets us to buy from them. So we have a lot of shit, and they get money. So what's in the ad that's going to get this car even if we had the money? How they fuck us over here? Excuse my language, Murray.

Shavon assumed that most white actions were designed to take advantage of blacks through the use of hidden persuasion. She speculated on the commerce that enriched white men and disempowered blacks. She was beginning to see these ads and others as adversarial and manipulative. If she can see how the manipulation works, she may be able to raise her political consciousness and simultaneously sharpen her analytic skills. Quiana deepened the analysis:

We gotta car here and a Hollywood actor. I don't know who he is. He's not handsome to me, but maybe to whites. They all are in these ads, perfect white people, perfect white teeth, which tell you the ads are not about real people—fake people, fake white people. So there should be lots of faking. Murray calls it secrets. A big car, a big house, a big star—I get it. What do the movies think black pimps drive and Mike Tyson and any rich dude or business man—a big car, a big man. Get it—a macho dude, plenty of money, plenty of women? Does this ad tell you that if you buy this car you will be a big man and get all the ladies you want?

I pointed out that in many ads an object like a car or a part of an object (like a seat or the car interior), or part of a human body (a breast or a crotch)—each one of these may symbolize something else or convey some secret message. So we had two objects: a car and leather seats. And we had Montalban stroking. Nathan, who took a later course in which we analyzed the same ad, extended the analysis:

Big car, big man—you mean big car, big dick. The car stands for the sex organ of the driver. Right? You mean that these guys drive big cars because they think woman think they big in bed? Does the car represent a penis? And when this guy strokes the car, he is really stroking a penis. And exciting women—who watch. I bet the whole thing is about sex.

Cherie, another transient, kept shaking her head, increasingly angry and shocked, "You're crazy, You're crazy, You think everything is sex." Cherie was one of the few deeply religious girls at Egleston who remained tied to the evangelical faith of her parents. She had no doubt about the Second Coming and Paradise. Her faith was firm. She believed that God directs man in ways that are always good even though the surface of life may appear to be irrational and cruel. Almost all the kids at Egleston say God exists. Many girls say God is their personal protector. Almost no one, however, goes to church or participates in any church-sponsored activities. God seems to be a totem to whom lip service is paid, a formulaic knee jerk, a deferential bow to pious parents. At one moment, a student will affirm God's existence and a moment later will say with anger, "If God existed, would we be here?"

Cherie was offended by an explicitly sexual interpretation and would not stop complaining: "You are crazy with all that talk. You think everything is sex. Well, it ain't. There is a God, and he is good, and he watches over. And this stupid ad has nothing to do with sex. It's about a car."

Robert ignored Cherie as if she were some petty annoyance, unworthy of his attention: "I don't understand the seats and the stroking." No one offered Robert any help so I asked more questions: "What do you do in a seat?"

"Sit down," Wanneta said as if I were stupid.

"So you sit in a seat in a big car that tells people what? And Montalban strokes the hood of the car and sits in the seat and talks about soft leather." Everyone looked troubled—the seat, the car, the hood, the stroking.

"I got it," Robert exclaimed. "The car not only tells people the driver's got a big penis and is a big man, the car itself is a penis, the whole thing is about sex. Right, right—seating, being seated, mounted. A man mounted in a soft seat."

Everyone yelled and laughed, and Shavon yelled, "Crazy, crazy, Murray, have you gone mad? You have a dirty mind." She smiled and said, "We are not going to lunch anymore with a dirty old man." Everyone was shrieking and laughing, but they were thinking about the meaning of the ad. Robert completed the puzzle:

The car is a man and a male organ, and the car is a woman that man gets into—that's the seat. So the ad appeals to men and woman, to their sex. These ads get people sexually up and interested without their knowing it.

Wanneta added, "And the car is money and power. The ad says, buy this car, and you can get a man or woman and be a big dude."

The class was not just analyzing one ad on television. Students were learning about symbols and double meanings and hidden persuasion. And most important, they were beginning to see how vulnerable they were to this double talk. And everyone was beginning to realize that they were looking at a heavily sexualized message that was designed to sell cars but had little to do with their quality. This little exercise, which seemed like innocent fun, a bit of comic, psychological serendipity, was actually poignant pedagogy for the students because it reminded them of how susceptible we were. We learned that day that the powerful prosper by tapping the language of hidden desire:

How am I going to know who is speaking to me and what he wants from me when everything is in a secret code? I told you before that nothing is what it looks like, you call it illusion and reality. There's got to be two worlds, straight and with symbols. It's like sellers and buyers. The white sellers use straight talk with each other and symbol double talk to us. We are victims of the economy, and we are victims of language.

The kids were gradually piecing together a universe in which the white world makes and sells while the black and Latino world contrives and consumes. They see a world beyond their control. They have become sophisticated enough to understand that language is itself a form of power, another tyranny they have to confront. In the process of coming to know the white world, the kids learned a bit about linguistics and a lot about manipulation.

It was time for us to move from learning how needs are fabricated to learning how candidates are marketed. The issue again was illusion and reality:

Elections change nothing. We are no better off no matter who is elected. Doesn't matter. They are out for themselves, not us. They come at election time and then, bang, they are gone. Besides, the real power not in the government. It's in the big money, the big dudes in the corporations, and the drug money. Not affected by our elections.

Since the political alienation of our kids, and for that matter the nation at large, is so pervasive, I introduced the theory of the alienated voter, which I had formulated in the 1960s to explain exotic and very negative voting behavior. I described how long-term corruption in Massachusetts and poor and costly public services had led voters to conclude that all politicians were crooks and that therefore it made no difference who won elections. I spoke about how voters use gut reactions to evaluate candidates since they believe all politicians lie: "I looked in his eyes and I knew he was a crook." I spoke about how voters feel alienated from their rightful political role as creators of responsible government. Everyone in our class understood because these kids knew from their experiences that the traditional civics class had little to do with reality.

So during the winter term of my third year, we read sections of interviews I had conducted with political candidates, political consultants, pollsters, and campaign managers during the past forty years. These men and women had managed eleven presidential campaigns, hundreds of congressional and gubernatorial campaigns, and dozens of mayoral contests. They had also managed campaigns in South America, Europe, and Asia.

I selected interviews taken during and after the Bush-Dukakis election that graphically describe how Bush and his consultants exploited racism via Willie Horton and created the illusion that Dukakis was weak on crime and a radical. I felt these kids could benefit from a look at Willie Horton, of whom they never heard, and from some familiarity with the code words used to bolster prejudice. Since a political campaign is a struggle for power in a highly competitive and amoral setting, not unlike life in Egleston Square, it seemed to be a potentially interesting topic for us.

I described what political consultants do, and the kids read from my interviews with Lee Atwater and Roger Ailes, two of the most skilled Republican strategists, architects of the Bush campaign and of much Republican strategy since Reagan. They also read excerpts from two interviews with a Democratic consultant who advised Dukakis to attack Bush and defend himself.

Rita quickly grasped a similarity in life style between consultants and kids in the neighborhood:

Man, these guys could be us, sneaking and plotting. All these consultants surrounding the man, that's a gang. They protect each other and plan together to kill the opponent. They got weapons, we got weapons. They got those code words, they got polls, they got psychologists. We got our wit and brothers and weapons, and we use psychology. They got a war, we got a war.

The consultants dealt with problems the kids could relate to: mobilizing manpower, isolating enemies, exploiting hatred. The dimensions are totally different, but the building blocks are similar. Political consultants evaluate strategic alternatives just as these kids had to think about alternative routes to and from school. The campaign to elect a president became a Darwinian model of the students' own struggle for survival. The interviews were "interactive," full of unsolved puzzles and possibilities that the kids tried to solve. They "became" political consultants in their own right.

Wanneta realized that Dukakis's refusal to defend himself was a fatal mistake (an opinion shared by the political consultants):

This dude in for big trouble because he thinks he is God. He think he is so pure voters won't believe that he really could be bad. The first thing you learn here is defend yourself, no matter who attacks you, defend yourself. Because if you don't, you look weak, and everybody will believe you are a wimp. Especially if you're running for president, I would tell the man to always fight back.

Robert was fascinated by the theories of this Dukakis advisor because they exposed how ad men excite and exploit sexual feelings to sell products and get votes. The consultant had worked with advertising agencies where he had developed a reputation for creating brilliant and offbeat ads. I once asked him what the greatest achievement of political consultants was. Without hesitation, he answered, "The Cold War, the greatest boogeyman in American history." Robert began to read aloud from the interview:

"Madison Avenue believes that the persuasiveness of television has absolutely nothing to do with words or the conscious meaning of pictures, but with finding out what it is that moves people psychologically and pressing those hot buttons in insidious ways so people don't know what you're doing. The Republicans are beginning to find that out. Television is not a literal medium. It appeals to emotions. The ad agency's approach is strictly Freudian. I sat through meetings with psychiatrists, sociologists, galvanic skin response experts, laser eye-beam movement experts, phallic shape and color experts, looking for ways to convince our target viewers that if he drinks our beer, he'll get better hard-ons. It had nothing to do with the product."

Robert read these few sentences again, very slowly. The girls laughed at the link between beer and hard-ons. Robert warned the other kids that they could easily become animals in some white experiment:

You got these galvanic skin guys and laser guys trying to find out what makes your skin get hot or your eyes move so they can push buttons and make us jump. They are trying to find out what makes us tickle, not what's good for us. We are like animals in an experiment. If they can make us get a hard-on, they can do anything with us.

The class was silent, faces troubled and frowning. Robert reminded the others: "This guy has more to say. We talked about Willie Horton last week, the black man Dukakis let out for a weekend, who raped a white woman. Many talked about the meaning of this."

Robert was now teaching our class and preparing the kids for another shock. I always had a very nice feeling when Robert took over. He was

about to introduce the consultant's analysis of the Willie Horton inci-
dent. He knew it provided an explosive and shocking example of how
racism is used by white politicians, a vivid confirmation of his conspiratorial views about American politics and life. The psychosexual innuen-
does of black rape as coaxed by Bush's advisors angered our class and
heightened the kids' awareness of the cavernous difference between
white and black. It was as if they had just been told they were lepers.
"Turn to page 13, I want to show you how we get fucked." Robert read
slowly, and everyone followed the words:

"If you don't take Bush out, immediately after the convention when you are
strongest, when you have lots of credibility, we are going to lose this election.
Because they are sending Willie Horton out to get you." O.K.? I cannot
think of a better scenario to psychologically target the male, blue-collar,
insecure, middle-aged man, suffering from performance anxiety, worried
about whether he can satisfy his wife or his girlfriend. I can't think of a
better scenario than to blame Michael Dukakis for a black man, who is
stronger than you, coming to your house, tying you up, and raping your
wife. The only worse thing I can think of is that he tied you up in the room
so that you had to watch and she liked it. This is how brutal this conversation got. What they want to say is that if you vote for Dukakis, a black man
will come to your house, he'll rape your wife, she'll like it, and he'll raise
your taxes. O.K.? That's what they want to say. They won't say that. They
can't say that. But they will find ways to say that on television. They will
find a code almost as powerful about the pledge to the flag. I said, "That's
coming. You've got to do a commercial about that. Right now. Where Mike
Dukakis comes out and says in front of a big flag, 'Nobody questions my
patriotism.' "

Shavon looked at Wanneta. Both were silent. Shandra shook her
head, and Robert was silent—for the moment. These kids had never

heard anything like these remarks. "What about these insecure blue-collar white men?" I asked. "Why can't they perform? Why can't they satisfy their girlfriends?"

We don't have that trouble. I told you the white world was fucked up. These men are wimps. You think black people or Latinos be crippled with performance anxiety? Who ever heard of performance anxiety? The whole idea sounds weird. Is it possible that their sex worries are caused by they so busy making money and so put down by the boss or the girlfriend? That the whites have such a crazy world. You think when people make slaves of others, it makes them nothing men. Wouldn't this make a man guilty and not able to have good relations with anyone? Maybe owning slaves and treating minorities like slaves makes the slave owner a bad person—he becomes bad, a gangster, he becomes the way he treats others, a murderer.

Wanneta was the first student I ever heard to speculate on the debilitating effects of slavery on masters. She was playing with the idea that one becomes what one does. Wanneta suggested that the master-slave relation dehumanizes the master as well as the slave, a recapitulation of Hegel's famous dialectic. But Wanneta broadened her theory. She believed that frantic money making and greed made white men anxious and crazy and impotent. Her thinking had matured. She was thinking in large structures—the economy, master-slave relations, dehumanization—and seeing connections between them.

At the same time, Wanneta's view of white society as frantic and sick led her to an elevated view of black culture:

Blacks may be poor and uneducated. But we are not crazy, and we are not frightened of sex. We are sisters and brothers. We got some love and pride and a community. The word *sister* means something to me.

Shavon started to laugh:

Murray, look around here. Sex everywhere. Babies, half the girls in the
school have babies. And if you counted fathers, look at Robert. We be easy
about sex and not afraid. It's whites who can't do it.

I asked the class to look at the consultant's comments about Willie
Horton once again. I wanted to talk about the role of anxiety and
politics: "Look at the words. Read the words carefully, and tell me why
is anxiety so important here for politics." Robert had no doubts:

Bush is trying to make whites anxious about blacks and Dukakis, and he is
using this very big emotion, this very big fear, to get votes. This is about
black men frightening white men. This is about getting people to change
by making them frightened. This is about using racism for politics.

I applauded Robert: "You are terrific. This is about using racism for
political gain, a tactic the Republicans have been using for twenty years.
And it has been very successful. Your answer is great as far as it goes, but
you are missing some details. The details often give us the deeper
meaning. Why 'insecure middle age men who are blue collar'? Why
performance anxiety? Do you know what blue collar means? And then
there is the very strange remark—'he tied you up so that you had to
watch and she liked it.' This is where part of the real meaning, the deep
meaning, is."
Shavon began to talk about love and fear:

This whole business is based on fear, fear of a big giant black man, fear of
his sexual might. Murray, this man understands that fear and love rule the
world, and if you can't get love, you'll get fear. I think people don't think so
good when they are afraid.

Wanneta interrupted, jumping and waving her hand, always eager to talk as if she had the final word, a blockbuster that illuminated the problem and made it clear that there was little else to be said. And she asserted herself with so much charm that no one took offense:

But this fear, this anxiety, not only makes people emotional and crazy, it makes them be weak and alone. You know how you feel on the "T" [public transport] late at night, scared. What do alone people want? Somebody to hang with. They need someone, like a baby, so they want to connect.

Wanneta had never read a book about politics, never thought about the role of anxiety in politics until this moment, never been exposed to the idea of charisma. Yet she anticipated some of the most profound insights of political sociology as she juggled the ideas of anxiety, fear, aloneness, and bonding in remarkable ways. Wanneta understood that anxiety makes people feel weak, alone, highly emotional, and therefore less rational and more available to politicians who can reduce their anxiety.

Shandra must have been moved by this talk of racism and Willie Horton because she began to talk sternly, full of rage:

What kind of man is Bush to do this with Willie Horton? A racist, a cheap racist. His life must be full of hate. You get mixed up with this shit, and this is what happens to you. How can you get millions of people to hate and be afraid.

Wanneta ended our class:

You get them afraid of a group that's different and get them to hate, and then promise you get rid of that group. Educate everybody to believe that blacks are murderers, that they hate you and will destroy you. Telling everybody how dangerous they are, so you need a big man to destroy them. We are very useful to white people. They unite to hate us.

◡

Thought as a Weapon

I know why Murray chooses the reading. Because it shows us something big about American life—how people fuck us and how political consultants use blacks to frighten whites. He wants us to see the secret world where power men work. He wants us to think about who we are and why we do something. He wants us to learn the methodology and to know ourselves. To know the world better. When we really know about causes and effects and systems, then we can think clearly. I like his idea that thought is a weapon.

I taught the kids at Egleston School that thought is a weapon, a key to their passage. And I taught this every week. I told them that their ability to see through the illusions that imprisoned them was a more powerful weapon than any other they might possess. They learned that knowledge is power and that no one has that power until they conquer the subject, know the contradictions and conflicts that fracture and force change. I urged the kids to examine their own lives and think very carefully about what motivates them. We listened to the pathos of the ghetto, the crises that turn lives: fathers abandoning their children, jealous boyfriends abusing women, unwanted babies, alcohol and drug addictions. And we talked about how they tried to handle these troubles. We spoke about these calamities as if we were doing social science. We talked about the probable causes of the trouble, the options we had, and the ways we might have behaved differently.

In retrospect, I realized we operated on several levels. We were studying social science—that is, learning about the world. And we were clarifying the concepts we used to analyze the world. We were applying our methodology. We were studying politics and psychology and becoming more self-conscious and politically aware.

I decided to teach kids how to think because they needed to know. It was that simple for me. I audited math and humanities classes at Egleston, and it was obvious that most of the kids who had trouble simply could not organize and process material logically. There was a lot of confusion about sequences and causation, much confusion about how characters in short stories used the past to predict the future or why A plus B must produce C. It was clear to me that our school, probably all schools, was teaching material and getting poor results because the logic was absent.

Periodically when we could not deal with a problem in class, I asked Janine or Rita how they resolved similar problems in their lives. Why are kids so thoughtful and logical about survival and so inadequate in school? Urban high schools should build on these strengths. Kids can learn to transfer these skills. They have spent years learning how to infer from past behavior, and they have become expert at integrating and processing large amounts of information relevant to survival, information that is often more complex than school work. I supplied my students with simple rules for thinking about society, and it made a substantial difference. I assumed they would learn something about history and politics in the process.

I decided that our projects had to be relevant in some really big way to life in the hood and helpful to kids who were trying to learn more about themselves. The most important decision teachers make concerns what shall be taught. I decided to provide my kids with a "political" education, not a partisan education or a provocative education but an education in the classical sense, an extensive discussion about what constitutes a good life and what impedes it.

Our discussion of who profits from the ghetto is a perfect example. One student talked about two policemen who were paid five thousand dollars a week to stay away from particular streets where cocaine was sold and to help if someone on the street was in trouble with the law. We had achieved a degree of sophistication so that everyone understood we were analyzing a system of buyers and sellers, an illegal system of needs and gratification, that required pacification of the police. Janine suggested that the system favors buyers because they have the capital to sustain themselves over time, whereas sellers seek immediate gratification and cannot bargain efficiently.

Wanneta talked about landlords charging high prices, although she had no idea that prices relate to supply and demand. I told them about markets, competition, and prices, and reminded them that it is useful to think in terms of needs, gratification, and scarcity. "We got no hope, so we got lots of storefront churches. Hope is a product that sells because demand is big, and that is what dope does, it gives hope, and that is what the church does."

"We got little money and bad credit and no banks," Rita remarked, "so we got check-cashing stores. That is our demand and their supply."

Shavon, who thought a lot about the outer fringes, the space where less imaginative kids never go, addressed me:

Hon, you have a job only because there is a ghetto. You profit because your book is about the joys of knowing us. The whole school profits from the ghetto because it wouldn't be here without the welfare workers and the social workers and the government people who have jobs dealing with us, even if it's just sending our checks. No poor people, no ghetto, no school.

Kanil, a boy who would have little trouble in college if he could mobilize himself, mentioned the unusually large number of used-car lots that ring Egleston Square and the four or five garages within three blocks that repair cars:

If it's cheap and it breaks, they sell it to us. We are the market for cheap surplus goods. We can only afford cheap cars so they are always getting repaired. In the end, we pay more, so mechanics profit. And washing machines and dryers we can't afford, so we pay each time we do washing. The people, they are like vultures who wait for us. When we sink, they rise. We demand cheap, they supply. It's a system.

Rita intoned, almost in a whisper as if she were reciting prayers for the dead:

I never thought of Roxbury or Dorchester like this, buyers, sellers, and poverty. I see now it's weak and strong because we weak become meat for the strong. That is your system, Murray, things defined by weak and strong. But this ain't where it stops. They profit from us when they need us to clean. We supply the unskilled, and they demand.

This was a remarkable session. The predatory nature of the ghetto became obvious to us. And we became adept at using our mini-systems analysis. The kids actually used many of the categories we developed in class: buyers and sellers, need and satisfaction, supply and demand, pacification. The students actually thought about the political economy of the ghetto as if it were a system of reciprocal needs operating within a larger economy, the hospital and McDonald's; they understood that these economic relations turn on the fulcrum of weak and strong.

This little case study, simplistic as it is, can be used as a model for alternative schools or any high school. Why not develop case studies like this one, or games and puzzles that provoke kids and take advantage of their imagination? Why not play "Utopia," a wonderful dreamlike game in which a community is lost at sea, then permitted to locate anywhere? The group must discuss how they will make decisions, how they will create an economy, what moral and religious prescriptions will be established, and so forth. The discussion exposes assumptions about community and privacy, ethics and power, and may even illuminate the origins of prejudice. "Utopia" can be a very rich experience if the teacher uses the Socratic method and forces students to reexamine cherished values.

These kids need projects that are exciting, projects that build on the supple intellectual strength of their street smarts, projects that force them to think and solve problems rather than accumulate knowledge. I assumed that if I could get kids to categorize and infer, to think systematically, they would enjoy life and school more because they would see more. I remember the social science teacher with whom I interned. He demanded that kids learn the name of the Massachusetts state flower and the number of state representatives and senators. He asked them to memorize the date when the state house was built. That teacher should have asked them to interview state representatives and ask why industries that contribute heavily to campaigns tend to benefit, why public utilities contribute primarily to committees that regulate electric and gas prices, or why incumbents invariably raise more campaign funds than challengers do. He should have focused on *process* and *power*, or how and why candidates decide to allocate funds, stress particular issues and ignore others, lie, debate or not debate. He should have taught students why voters are alienated and how candidates develop strategies designed to reduce their alienation. He should have raised the ultimate political issue—how meaningful is democracy in America? These kids are excited by *reality,* not fairy tales.

These kids live in a world where survival often depends on a precise reading of reality. Their life is an oral history of signals understood and cues misinterpreted. The analysis of Bush and Willie Horton caused a riot of indignation. Our study of population and aggression produced a contest to locate the source of India's pacificity. When Shavon connected Martin Luther King and Gandhi with nonviolence, everyone applauded.

School must be experienced as a renaissance, a chance to be born again. Events take place there that thrill and change life forever. Is it possible that a few kids kill each other because the act is transcendent, an ultimate experience, pathological but so shocking that it forever changes the shooter and the victim? Violence can be redemptive, apocalyptic, an orgasm beyond compare, the revocation of nihilism. Why not make school a redemptive and life-giving place?

School must be breathtaking, literally breathtaking. The kids need to feel vibrant; they must be moved, shaken, dazzled, shocked back to life. And that is why it is necessary to study great ideas, big theories, grand events. Basic skills cannot be omitted, but we should be teaching the great ideas that have changed history. We need a miniversion of the curriculum used at the University of Chicago or St. John's. Why not study math and science with a model of James Watt's steam engine? Why not look at the principles behind the mechanism and try to infer the process by which Watt imagined how to put principles into practice? We might even try to improve his machine. We could also look at the enormous impact the steam engine had on the industrial revolution. Some boys are amateur auto mechanics. Watt's machine would be a solid teaching tool for them. To prepare kids for the world, we must teach how computers affect employment, how technology changes politics and morality. We should talk about ancient ethical issues. Why not have a mock-up of the Ten Commandments and debate when one might rightfully violate a commandment. Shalt thou steal when thy parents are starving? Shalt thou kill thy mother when she has sexually abused you? These are real issues in the ghetto.

For three years, we talked about issues like these, ones rarely raised in urban high schools. Our discussion of how advertising appeals to the unconscious led to talk about Freud and the unconscious and dreams. We talked about the big bang and the Cold War, but we also talked about what makes men aggressive and how societies curb aggressivity. We talked about tension management and the conditions for democracy. I let the talk move wherever the kids wanted it to go. I wanted to take advantage of their enthusiasm, and I knew we could learn about systems and conflict and change regardless of the issues. I hoped they would understand that everything, including themselves, is in process and that what finally transpires is usually a truncated version of what could have been. I wanted them to appreciate the concept that an acorn is best defined as an oak tree. For us, process became a critical idea.

Large issues stretch these students and make them realize that school is important. Many Egleston kids define themselves in part by how seriously their teachers take them. They know when something important is on the table and they respond. The kids were different after they discovered Willie Horton. The girls in particular became irritable. They spoke of Bush with much hatred: "Where does all the hate come from?" The students will not forget Willie Horton and the work we did on anxiety and politics. This lesson was precisely what I wanted it to be, relevant to daily life and useful for understanding a very important political type, the demagogue who achieves power by mobilizing anxiety.

In addition to solid training in math and science, literature and history, these kids also need projects that teach the symbolic and manipulative language that floods American politics and advertising. I wanted my students to know when they are manipulated and how they are moved without their will and against their will. I wanted my class to know how and why a culture of consumption exists. I wanted my class to think about how power is achieved and how they might use it to change their lives. The curriculum had to be political because our kids cope with power every day—the arbitrary power of parents, the power of racist police, the power of teachers who dislike them, and the power of rival gangs. And the kids must deal with the power of a market which has little space for them. These kids must therefore study history, not as a parade of comings and goings, but as a series of conflicts and compromises about power. They must learn to identify the agents of change and the forces that promote stability.

Educators and politicians object to "politics" in the public schools although the public school system is the most important vehicle in our culture for indoctrinating kids in the virtues of free enterprise and electoral politics. The argument that schools are not political is ridiculous. The schools not only affirm the American way, they often replicate the existing division of labor and preserve the class system.

I learned during my first year at Egleston that the kids need primary sources that are vivid and authentic—tape recordings, interviews, correspondence. The students were excited and angry when they read interviews with former slaves, but they couldn't read Zinn's chapter on slavery. They read excerpts from my interview with the Republican strategist, Lee Atwater, and were angered by his plans for isolating the opposition and defining it as deviant and dangerous. They understood that they were victims of that strategy. But they won't or can't read a book about political campaigning. So we often read aloud and role-played. As mentioned before, I always assigned the most important roles to the least-involved kids. Their appointment became a badge of honor that brought them back to us and made them feel good. I remember the day when "Khrushchev" screamed at "Kennedy" and told him that Russia would destroy the United States. Everyone backed off. I remember the girl who screamed, "Oh my God," when the "secretary of defense" presented this awesome scenario. We all knew that John Kennedy would not back down. His voice left no doubt. Nothing could have been more real. The kids in "First Person History" transformed themselves for a bit and "suffered" through the crisis.

I also learned that students can radically improve their ability to think critically in a matter of months. They must be prepped in geography and history to repair the damage done by the schools and the ghetto. They must do remedial work in vocabulary, and they must meet in small classes and be tutored with affection and discipline. The setting must be intimate. The kids must be called on at every session. They must read aloud and, above all, they must not be made ashamed to plead ignorance.

I believe that urban high schools need to be more like elementary schools and they need to be much smaller. There should be more communal activities with teachers, parents, and administrators where kids can talk about school and themselves—more lunches, more trips to museums and ball games, visits to historic places, a track-and-field day, more yoga and Tai Chi, a course in parenting, trips to factories and fairs, and a visit downtown to see how the world works. These are the times when the teacher becomes a companion. These activities may seem peripheral, but they are essential to the business of educating alienated and withdrawn kids who need to bond and trust before they become interested in school and believe it is relevant. The school must be a trusting and affirming friend, or it will fail. Classes must become community enterprises, places where kids want to be, where talk about "the brothers" has real meaning.

I am certain that resurrection is possible. The minds of these kids have not atrophied. They can be reached; they can be taught to think abstractly and with subtlety; and they can master rules for doing social science. Our approach was rudimentary compared with a decent freshman college course, but it was very sophisticated for high school. When my students needed help, I gave it to them, but I never supplied answers, only questions. I did not use inspirational literature about Latino and black heroes. I told them every day that we were doing important work and insisted that the theory they learned would enable them to see more and farther. They learned that theory is very practical. They saluted me with the high level of their work, and I responded by refusing to lower standards.

I got what I gave. The respect these kids crave can only be given by teachers who ask for more. When the students in "First Person History" realized we were dealing with intriguing material, they thanked me by going to class and trying. I remember the poignant moment when Kathy answered a difficult question, and I praised her for her marvelous answer. She looked at me incredulously and asked, "Do you really mean it? Was it good? Was my answer good?" I told her that she was terrific and her answer was very helpful to us. She jumped up, big smile, gorgeous brown eyes, and started to applaud herself. Everyone joined in as if a great event had occurred. It was a great event. Kathy chose that day, I think, to assert her intention to live.

As I said in the beginning, the bond which created a community of learners for us was sealed at our lunches when Marieca, Robert, Shavon, Douglas, Jorge, Janine, Kathy, Alourdes, Rita and the others revealed themselves. Lunch was our most important "academic" exercise, the time when trust began, the moment when our class decided to learn.

We lunched together every month, and we talked a lot after class. We talked about who we loved, who we lost, and how it hurt. One girl told me what motherhood was like at eighteen, how lonely and frightening it was without the father. Some girls spoke with bitterness about the boys who imprisoned them within walls of accusation and jealousy. But they also spoke a lot about the unconditional love of grandmothers or aunts who raised them, or older sisters who protected them and taught them the art of self-protection. They talked about crime, theirs and that of the police.

I told them about my wife's experience in jail during the civil rights movement and how she was persecuted at the dining table of her French grammar school because she refused to eat the rotten, smelly cheese that only the French seem to love. I told them about the antics of my ten-year-old son who asked me if I knew who Mr. Albert Einstein was. I told him. At which point, he said, "Move over, Albert," and handed me his A+ science paper, which gravely reported that worms move away from intense heat. Everyone at the table laughed and sensed how much I love my boy.

They were most interested in my oldest son, who works for the Rolling Stones, and wanted to know if I could get free tickets to concerts for them. I told them how frightened I was when I entered Harvard College, barely seventeen, and how inadequate I felt when I listened to boys in class much brighter than me. I described my heart attack and triple-bypass surgery and the abyss I felt when I thought of leaving everyone I love. I also told them how they had changed my life.

I had tried to teach my students how to think so that they can more easily know themselves and what it is that hems them in. And the results were remarkable, troubled kids with absolutely no education, no history, and no psychology talking about the uses of anxiety in politics and predicting Khrushchev's behavior. But these were successes. I continue to think about the kids who refused to learn, the kids who were shot and abused, the kids who were high and drunk and depressed. I have realized that what we did together was wonderful, but it was also very little: twelve or fifteen kids in the midst of millions who can barely manage to get to these gigantic factory schools that only magnify their alienation. I had students who barely came to class, who dropped my class, who dropped out of school.

Many Egleston kids are still dead in spirit. They still accept their place as if it were part of some universal order, sanctified by the god of inevitability. They still behave as if tomorrow will replicate today. There is still a timeless quality about their outlook, a sense that little matters and nobody is going anywhere. No one rushed to class when I arrived, and no one crowds the corridor today. Dozens of Egleston students have been unaffected by school.

In spite of all the talk about rich and poor, we and they, the powerful and the powerless, despite all the talk about the corruption of the state and its manipulation by the rich, despite all the talk about genocidal conspiracy by the government to kill blacks with AIDS and drugs, most of the kids know little or nothing about their history. Martin Luther King is a relic of the dim past—a faint memory. Malcom X is more contemporary, a more violent voice, perhaps more their style, but they don't really know what he preached. Farrakhan is the only black political figure they recognize, and no one mentions him except when he speaks in Boston.

I emphasize once more that these kids have no legacy, no consciousness of the giants in their past. They need skills, but they also need instruction that deals with the ancient dialectic, power and powerlessness, exploiter and exploited, change and stability, servitude and liberation.

I hope that our work will help Robert and Wanneta and Marieca do well. Yet I am not optimistic. Though the Greater Egleston Community High school survives, the school and the cruel ghettos of Boston move at cross-purposes. The political economy of Boston and this country creates the poverty and indolence of the ghettos, which in turn produce our students. Misguided educators believe that schools can change the lives of millions of black and Latino kids. They have reversed the natural order. When the economy begins to serve true human needs, the school will produce responsible and engaged human beings.

〜

A Note to Teachers Who Want to Change the World—Student by Student

The pedagogy developed at the Greater Egleston Community High School was based on the logic and theories of knowledge developed by Plato and Aristotle and refined for centuries by philosophers concerned with cognition. The ability to conceptualize and apply learning to new and different domains is the tool that makes it possible for students to use their imaginations productively in the anatomy of scholarship. Good teachers train students to master a discipline. Great teachers alter the dynamics of their students' cognition and enlarge their capacity for logic.

I could have used the Socratic method, always asking questions, rarely supplying answers, with suburban or urban fourth or eighth graders. I could have taught them to recognize causes and effects, to identify and analyze systems, and to appreciate process. I had done this with inner-city kids. Although my students were black, Latino, urban, and not affluent, the platonic pedagogy—learning how to think systemically and recognize patterns and forces that promote or hinder change—is critical for students regardless of race, ethnicity, or class. As teachers, we may have to supply more- or less-sophisticated techniques with children of different backgrounds, but the categories—cause, effect, system, stability, conflict, and change—are proven to be useful in all disciplines, for students of any grade, and for teachers who want their students to think clearly.

I greatly underestimated the potential of Egleston kids when I first arrived. They seemed to be interested only in immediate gratification and saw no future. School was therefore irrelevant and pointless. Their discussion about who creates history, however, was so impressive that it made me think about the potential that lay dormant in these kids. In my mind, Egleston became a school with high standards, where my insistence on quality work was the norm. I realized this was a fantasy, a vision perhaps, more than a reality. But several critical decisions that I made were strongly affected by this vision.

The utility and beauty of learning depend on appreciating the wider connections and possibilities contained in an elegant geometrical proof or a poignant short story. Until students understand the linkages that create a system—the essential elements that make an organic whole—they will not be able to address the basic question of science or the humanities: Why? *Why* did Napoleon attack Russia? *Why* do some people rely on magic rather than science? *Why* can scientists predict the existence of unknown elements or black holes that can never be observed? *Why* do some nations become totalitarian and others democratic? *Why* did Khrushchev send missiles to Cuba? Teachers must make it absolutely clear to students that no issue is really settled, no answer is really sufficient, unless students can explain why the phenomenon itself occurred. Teachers must impress upon students the subtlety of these issues by demonstrating how definitions determine the findings. The salient question is always *why*.[1]

I urge teachers to create courses that require students to compare, contrast, and develop wider connections. Have your students analyze two or three historical events, short stories, or mathematical theorems that appear to be very similar but produce unexpected and quite different outcomes. Create lesson plans that require students to locate and explain the deviant case: fictional characters, for example, who suddenly behave profoundly out of character or revolutions that produce results very different from those intended. The challenge for students is to identify the unpredictable by locating the idiosyncratic forces. This, of course, is one of the first steps in science, and an exercise that sharpens logic.

I learned the value of analyzing the deviant case at Egleston when I asked students to relate the population of five nations to their propensity for war. Among the nations we selected, India, at that time, seemed to be relatively passive in its foreign relations compared with Germany, Russia, Japan, and the United States. Students developed several of the classic arguments about why countries with large populations or limited land masses would be aggressive. But they could see no reason why India, with a very large population, was relatively passive. Because teachers should provide assistance only when the students have exhausted their resources, I suggested that Martin Luther King had learned much from Gandhi—that is all. Two or three students knew about Gandhi's passive resistance, and they quickly perceived that India, with its huge population, had a strong tradition of pacifism. Whether they were correct is not as significant as the fact that they could recognize deviance and realize that ideas can greatly affect the course of history.

It is important that you frequently stress the fact that thought is a weapon and support this by providing many examples. This alerts students to the value of a solid education. Ask them to read any book that uses thought as a weapon to invent the steamboat, or the phonograph, or the telephone, or to resolve a great scientific mystery. Ask your students to read *The Double Helix*, by James Watson and Francis Crick, who mapped the structure of DNA, solving, through reason, one of the great mysteries of science. Thought was their weapon. Your class may appreciate that school is a critical place where students are taught to use thought as a weapon. It is important for you to find books, articles, or diaries in which inventors and scientists describe the mental processes they went through to achieve their objective. It is always helpful to supply examples.

I urge teachers to abandon chronology in favor of comparative studies. Teachers must train students to realize that the causes of growth and decay are the essential components of comparative analysis. The rich texture of the past and present becomes palpable when comparative literature or history is the issue. Perspectives are enriched; the uniqueness and commonality of institutions are exposed. Ask your students to compare America in the sixties and in the nineties. Ask your students to read a few sermons delivered by Puritan divines in the seventeenth century and contrast their views on sin and salvation with those of contemporary Unitarian ministers or southern Baptists. The change and continuity of America's moral compass will become evident and the students' understanding of American history will deepen.

Examine ancient imperial societies—Egypt, Rome, or Greece—and, more recently, Russia under Stalin and Great Britain during the Victorian era. Ask your students to determine how ancient and contemporary elites pacified their masses. Responsible teachers of civics and American or world history must discuss how societies and governments legitimate themselves. They must teach why ideological indoctrination through school, church, and the media is more efficient and subtle, less costly, and barely noticeable compared with terror. Students in America are entitled to know that the great problem of American industry was not to produce more commodities, but to produce

more consumers. This is one key to understanding how American
citizens have been turned into consumers and why the shopping mall
is now the archetypal American institution. It is also a key to understanding that political candidates are merchandised like candy or soap.

Students are entitled to know how and why consent is manufactured, not because the idea implies a radical perspective but because
consent *is* manufactured, citizens have become consumers, and politics is marketing. Students' maturity and freedom depend on understanding this and reversing these trends. Courses that compare these
trends in different cultures are probably the last way to raise consciousness.

The fabric of history and literature is enriched through comparison
and contrast with Europe. We understand America with greater defi-
nition when we realize that feudalism and socialism, which shaped
much of European history, were absent in America. Students will feel
that unique quality of American history only when they realize that
political liberalism and free enterprise triumphed so completely because neither feudalism nor socialism was present to challenge America's fixation on unanimity. These insights about America become
meaningful only through comparison with Europe and Asia.

A comparison of the industrial revolution of the eighteenth century
and the information revolution of the late twentieth century could be
very rich. Teachers and students must first agree on what might be the
dynamic element—the energy and goals—of each revolution. This
question provides the first opportunity for serious discussion. The answer may well be "progress." But what are the criteria for measuring
progress—spiritual, material, cultural, scientific, the state of public
health, expanding self-consciousness? The question is useful because
it generates relevant questions that require students to make more
connections and think more systemically. How is progress mea-
sured—church attendance, gross national product, rates of crime and

divorce, literacy, infant mortality, equality? These are critical questions that teachers should raise, not merely because they are vital but because they also familiarize students with some important categories of social science, including causation, measurement, the nature of class and power, and zero-sum problems.

After the abstract questions (what is progress?) have been discussed, teachers should require specific answers to specific questions—preferably answers that are quantifiable; for example, changes in the distribution of wealth from 1750 to 1825, as compared with changes since the beginning of the information revolution. It is important for students to understand that quantification not only clarifies issues but also frequently resolves them. Ask your students to gather data on the quality of life of capitalists and workers during both revolutions. The question demands that students discuss the criteria appropriate for such a measurement: diet, longevity, housing, income, working conditions, political power, powerlessness, health care, social and economic mobility, and so on.

The selection of criteria can be a valuable lesson if students explain why one criterion is more meaningful than another. Locating data in libraries and learning how to use it provides students with additional skills. Wise and realistic teachers must suggest, but not demand, that certain lines of inquiry may be more fruitful. Students must locate, through trial and error, the domains worth studying. They may discover that the concepts of class and stratification are useful. They may, with some guidance, perceive the critical roles of technology, innovation, finance, education, and inheritance in determining who prospers and who does not.

Teachers dealing with progress as a generative topic should ask students to compare how societies during the industrial revolution legitimated great disparities of wealth and the authority of the state compared to the way it is done now in societies profoundly affected by the information revolution. The wise teacher may then suggest that ideas, myths, and religion may play a key role in the process. Ask your students to talk about what binds them to the American way and from whom they learned the routines of pacification or rejection. Comparative analysis that resonates with the realities of daily life is a valuable academic asset.

Because reality for many adolescents is television, I urge teachers to familiarize students with the power of images, the lingua franca of advertising and politics. Bill Moyers produced an intriguing one-hour documentary for PBS on the power of images in advertising and politics.[2] Moyers interviewed academics who specialize in communications and advertising executives who create commercials. Most of them suggested not only that we live in a universe of seductive images but also that the power of symbols and images is rapidly replacing language as a means of communication. One communications specialist suggested that Americans have been transformed from citizens into consumers. Politics, therefore, is merchandising, and candidates are commodities. Accompanied by class discussion, Moyers' video could entice your students to discuss media manipulation, the decline of participatory democracy, or, perhaps, the issue of free will.

Would it not be interesting to compare the primitive quality of advertising during the industrial revolution with the subtlety, seductiveness, and power of television and the Internet, which play such a large part in our students' daily lives? Teachers should use a discussion of the World Wide Web and, for example, TV's Home Shopping Network to introduce some of the most profound and dangerous changes in American life: the transformation of citizens into consumers, the replacement of language with images, and the effects these changes have on American politics and culture.

Your civics course and your course in American history are woefully archaic if you fail to deal with these dangerous and fundamental

changes. I urge you to prepare lesson plans that document the mergers
and acquisitions in the media, lesson plans that illustrate the concen-
tration of ownership of television and radio stations, newspapers,
magazines, the Internet, and Hollywood. Have your students discuss
the meaning of the Bill of Rights in a universe dominated by media
moguls. What does freedom of speech or of the press mean when
citizens have little or no access to the media? Are democracy and mo-
nolithic control of the media compatible? Some teachers might view
this agenda as an effort to radicalize students. It may be that, but I
think of it as an agenda designed to deal with reality. The transformation of citizens into consumers has profound implications for democracy.

I asked my students to watch the late-evening news on television
and keep a log of feature stories and descriptions of the ads. It did not
occur to me at that time to ask them to videotape the ads, but this
could be a fruitful approach. Several students concluded that the news
was not news but entertainment and commerce. Their logs were relatively faithful to the facts. The typical evening included a fire, a major
crime or sexual assault, an automobile accident, natural disasters, a
heroic act by man or dog, a bow to democracy in the form of a town
meeting filled with angry citizens, weather, and sports.

They understood the news was a series of sensational and mournful
images. They described the ads as serene or jarring, sexual, beautiful,
and enticing. But they could not move beyond these observations.
They did not realize, for example, that what appears on television is
frequently taken as truth, that television is "better" than reality—
more vibrant, more colorful, and more seductive. When the class has
exhausted its resources, it is time for teachers to intervene, the time
when the Socratic method is appropriate—questions, more questions,
and a little help. When we reached the "end," I asked my students
what they thought about while watching. The answers varied

greatly—anger, lust, hatred, a desire to punish the criminal or the drunk driver who killed a child, a desire to look as sensual as the models in the ads or as cool as the men driving the sports cars.

I was not interested primarily in individual feelings. I wanted to see whether my students had common reactions. I asked them to classify their reactions to see if there was a pattern, a dominant theme. I did this not merely to discover commonalities but to acquaint them with the process of classifying or categorizing seemingly idiosyncratic and random reactions. Classification is one easy way to bring order out of chaos, the first step that may improve students' ability to see patterns and connections, the first step toward thinking systemically and abstractly. Teachers, particularly elementary school teachers, should provide numerous examples of the dimensions frequently used to categorize—height, length, color, size, shape, velocity, intensity, universality, and so on. Teachers should create puzzles or games that demand classifications.

If I had required my students to classify their feelings, they might have deduced that the local evening news was designed to titillate them, to appeal to their sensate and voyeuristic needs—perhaps, on a deeper level, to appeal to their repressed sadism: accidents, murder, fire, child molestation, hurricanes, tornadoes. My students might have realized that the "news" occupies the space between ads that are often more vibrant and narcissistic than the news of the day, a suspicion that is played out in some of their reactions:

Yeah, I watch many hours every day. I love my programs. They let me forget all the shit at home and on the street. And sometimes I think I am a beautiful white model. I get lost with all the soap operas. Become the good girlfriend or the bad wife. I learn white ways, and I learn how wicked they are.

I watch TV because it excites me—mostly movies, *Rambo*, Steven Sea-

gal, *Terminator*. These guys know how to do it. How to blast their enemies, bang, bang, how to get exactly what they want, not afraid to shoot
or kill, not afraid to die. They could teach us plenty. You've got to *take*.
No one will give. Got to be ready to grab it.

Nobody believes me, but I like the ads sometimes better than the programs. The ads is beautiful, and they show me all the wonderful things I
could have if I was rich, which I ain't. I be poor, but I can dream.[3]

These questions and answers can lead students to more sophisticated vantage points. Ideally, each question will generate more questions and every answer will solicit additional answers. The generative
nature of these dialogues is clear. The dynamic invites students to deal
with the causation and increasingly larger connections between their
own experience and the topic under discussion.

Ask your students about their work experience. Ask them about
distribution of benefits to children by their parents. Ask them how
much time they spend watching television, studying, and shopping at
the mall. Have them describe the images on TV ads that appeal to
them. Find out who reads a daily newspaper. Ask them to interview
their parents, grandparents, and friends about their work and leisure.
Suggest that the shopping mall is now the critical American institution—not Congress, not the president, not the school. Do they think
this is reasonable? What would it signify for America if the mall were
the centerpiece of our culture? These questions relate to the original
issue—what is progress? Does progress resonate with their daily lives?

A comparative analysis of the industrial revolution and the revolution in information technology allows teachers to introduce critical
ideas of which American students are usually oblivious. One hundred
million Americans are now on-line, and the overwhelming majority
are white. Lack of access to computers can only widen the gap in
education between the majority and the minorities. Lack of access can

only reinforce class differences and condemn minorities to unskilled jobs and lower salaries, which would strengthen racist stereotypes.

Despite robotics and automated production processes, the alienation of labor continues. Millions of workers continue to perform repetitive and stultifying labor in jobs that chain them to their machines. They are dehumanized because their labor is not creative, not conducive to growth, not challenging. Workers do not control the choice of the commodities they create or the division of labor that facilitates production. Millions perform endless, repetitive, and mindless tasks. Their hands and fingers, figuratively speaking, become appendages of the machine they operate. While they are transformed into tools, they become reified, "toolized"—a joyless and uncreative cog in a vast and anonymous process.

The concepts of alienated labor and reification are not ideas commonly used by economists and historians who concentrate on wages, hours, productivity, and working conditions. Interest in the conditions of work, however, is not customarily framed in terms of alienation or reification. The concept of alienated labor is "un-American" but critical for understanding the relation of capital to labor today or in the eighteenth century. Teachers should introduce themselves and their students to these ideas, not merely because they are useful but because they are generative.

The concept of alienated labor invites discussion on the relation of teacher to student, parent to student, the nature of authority, power, powerlessness. Above all, teachers should turn the discussion to the need for young people to find creative, joyous, and unalienated labor. Alienation is also a fundamental concept for understanding contemporary politics—witness the tens of millions of alienated voters in America who feel powerless and without significant choices.

Ask your students to poll their neighbors, parents, and friends and ask the questions political scientists customarily use to measure political alienation: Do you agree or disagree:

- Nothing I do seems to have any effect upon what happens in politics.
- It seems to me that whoever you vote for, things go pretty much the same.
- No matter what people think, a few people will always run things anyway.
- My vote counts. We still have a government by consent of the people.
- I feel that my political leaders hardly care what people like myself think or want.[4]

If their results (substantial alienation) resemble hundreds of public-opinion polls taken since the sixties and designed to measure political efficacy, the results will generate significant questions: Why is political alienation so widespread? What is the effect of large-scale alienation on legitimacy? What might restore a sense of political efficacy? Does political alienation spawn right-wing groups? And so on. The generative quality of these issues is significant because political power and government by consent are fundamental issues. You must ask your students how the textbook on American history deals with alienation, if at all.[5]

Teachers should ask their students to think about the regressive implications of instant information as well as the liberating implications. Think of what the FBI or the KGB can do with their information. Think about what can happen to privacy. Ask your students to think about how the Internet greatly increases their ability to do scholarly work. After they affirm the Internet's facility to improve and accelerate scholarship, ask them whether research via the Internet creates problems of verification. If they do not respond, you may have to suggest that the Internet changes the notion of the "authority" and the integrity of sources. Students need to develop the ability to distinguish between reliable and unreliable sources: The appearance of data on the Internet does not carry the imprimaturs of truth.

Meaningful answers are possible only when students perceive the systemic nature of the problem. The best way to acquaint students with the nature of systems may be to require them to create one. A group of students at Egleston decided to "reinvent" the bathtub so that it was more user-friendly.[6] The students redesigned the flow of water by introducing spigots that pumped out dirty water and recycled it into clean water. They replaced metal tubs with an imaginary soft, warm plastic that vibrated and changed shape as the bather moved. They created a hydraulic system that energized their changes. They obviously understood some basic elements of hydraulics, and with this knowledge they created a system.

I urge teachers to visit science museums and factories where guides can describe operating systems and demonstrate how machines or robots work in synchronization. Most science museums have replicas of da Vinci's inventions or early versions of the printing press or the steam engine or clocks—all of which can be used to instruct students. Teachers should ask students to think about the effects of robotics on employment and the division of labor. The value of these trips would be greatly enhanced if students had an opportunity to talk to workers and learn about their satisfaction or alienation.

Beyond accumulated knowledge, such trips can become moments during which teachers and students bond, discover common interests, and learn to respect one another. The context of traveling in buses to museums or factories and eating and singing together creates a camaraderie not possible in a classroom. In *Teach Me!* I noted that students unburdened themselves during our lunches. It was a time when I learned to commiserate with my students, a time when our intimate conversations produced the mutual care and love that made my students want to perform well and made me increase my efforts to locate large and relevant issues for us to analyze. I believe that high school should be more like grammar school—more trips, more field days, more community.

It is important that you select critical historical moments for your students to analyze, moments of ferment and creativity, novels that changed literary traditions, science that broke new ground. Ask your high school science students to read Thomas Kuhn's *The Structure of Scientific Revolutions,* which will provide them with a clear idea of the conditions conducive to great advances in science. Familiarize your students with the thought processes, the logic scientists used to resolve some the greatest mysteries of the universe. This is also the time to familiarize your students with the fierce opposition to science by groups—mostly religious—who feel threatened. Good teachers deal simultaneously with science and the social context of science. This discussion leads naturally to a reiteration of the key idea—thought as a weapon.

Dozens of first-class books have been written for high school students on science and the social context of science. Assign *A Civil Action,* by Jonathan Harr, or Ibsen's great play *An Enemy of the People,* or *The Band Played On: Politics, People, and the AIDS Epidemic,* by Randy Shilts, all of which deal with the power of the law and society to frustrate or misuse science. Assign Steven Weinberg's *The First Three Minutes,* which deals with what occurred during the 180 seconds after the big bang. The book's argument does not require knowledge of the mathematics involved.

I underestimated the potential of my students during my first few months at Egleston. This was a grievous error. I suspect many teachers will assume these books are well beyond the capacity of their students. I catered to the lowest common denominator for months. My students responded by doing little work. When we bonded, when their anger and anxiety diminished, when they believed I was "with" them, they began doing homework and became eager to participate in class. Do not assume your students are beyond redemption. We have no idea of the core that lies under the superstructure created by television and our culture of consumption.

Do not lower your standards. Respect for teachers is essential to a disciplined and productive class, and so is respect for the potential of students. My students ultimately responded to big issues when they resonated with their daily life. My students were interested in the missile crisis because it reiterated the precarious balance between life and death in the ghetto. My students, who negotiate a gauntlet of potential misfortunes day after day, appreciated the negotiation process between Kennedy and Khrushchev—the issue of who may live and who may die. They reacted strongly to George Bush's exploitation of race and Willie Horton. The racism issue was obvious and personal. They loved to speculate about who owns the ghetto, and who controls the United States, because they know what it means to be powerless and how power is accumulated in the ghetto.

At this point, it may be wise to ask how we know whether students truly understand what we are teaching. Teachers must require that students apply what they have learned in one area to other areas and to new situations. Students must be able to explain why the application is meaningful. Teachers must require "performances of understanding" in the form of written work, artistic endeavors, scientific experiments, logical demonstrations, plays, paintings, and collaborative enterprises. Students understand when they can successfully apply a theorem in geometry to new and more sophisticated problems. The test is utilitarian.

I knew my students understood the power structure of the ghetto when they could define the reciprocal and mutually beneficial exchanges between the drug dealers and the police. They understood that the ghetto created jobs for social workers and opportunities for police brutality. They understood that a low-income community provides business opportunities for stores that cash checks, for Laundromats, for individuals who can translate, and for stores that sell prepaid cards for long-distance telephone calls. They understood that the ghetto is a delicate social system, and they knew why the power structure of the ghetto is unstable.

My students became increasingly sophisticated, and so will your students if you focus their attention on reciprocal roles and systemic analysis. Ask your students to read *Tally's Corner,* by Elliot Liebow, which beautifully describes the variety of roles played in a poor, black neighborhood. Ask your students to read *The Chrysanthemum and the Sword*, by Ruth Benedict, which deals with Japan's two distinct social systems: politeness and mutual respect (the chrysanthemum) and militaristic feudalism (the sword). Ask your students to write a systemic analysis of football, baseball, or soccer—all systems with well-defined roles that shift rapidly with changing conditions. If they can do this, you know they understand.

Suggest that democracy is a system in which voters are supposed to act rationally, vote in terms of self-interest, and familiarize themselves with the positions of candidates—who are supposed to act on their announced principles. Ask if this occurs in fact. Their responses will indicate whether they appreciate the malfunction of the American system and, perhaps, their own alienation.

Teachers should not be satisfied with accurate descriptions of a fictional character or social systems. Good teachers demand explanations of the underlying dissonance and harmony that excite change. The issue is process and potential. For my students, an acorn was not a small brown nut but an oak tree in the process of becoming. True knowledge resides in understanding—growth and decay, integration and disintegration. This is what I was trained to teach. This is what I wanted to teach. This is what I was capable of teaching. The study of process was our essential curriculum, but whenever possible we used primary sources and a comparative approach. These decisions, more than any other, determined what happened during my three years at Egleston.

I familiarized my students, for example, with the length and cost of American and British political campaigns, because the electoral process and public policy in America are profoundly affected by the sources of large campaign contributions, while the United Kingdom is relatively immune to campaign financing. A close reading of the process by which money filters through the American system accounts for much of what occurs inside the Beltway.

The comparison between America and England made the American case more striking. My students began to ask who makes large contributions, why they contribute and to whom, and what they get in return. I traced the pattern of giving to the congressional committees that were in a position to affect the business of the contributors. These patterns led several students to ask what power, then, do people have when they can't make significant contributions? Then the ultimate question: Is America a democracy or a plutocracy? These questions were provoked by the comparative analysis of the United States and Great Britain. My students were beginning to understand why thought is a weapon.

At some point, your class may need a wake-up call—it may be initiated by an inflammatory issue that cannot be resolved by traditional pedagogy, or by the indifference or hostility of your students, or by their brilliance or low test scores. These may be signs that it is time for you to review your work or change what you teach or how you teach.

My wake-up call occurred while we were talking about historiography. So many students made perceptive remarks about God as a cause of history, technology, great ideas, great men, or economic necessity. They even proposed the idea that history was too complicated to understand. I knew then that their potential was substantial—repressed by ghetto culture, but substantial. We had another wake-up call that made me realize the power of primary sources. I discussed George Bush's exploitation of Willie Horton and racism, designed to win southern support. I showed the infamous TV spot, which graphically shows unkempt and primitive-looking black men and an occasional white man exiting a revolving door—allegedly on furlough and on their way to rape white women. The fact that I could show a copy of that video in my class made Bush's racism graphic. The video is a primary source. Its power rests in its immediacy and authenticity. A student remarked, "This whole business is based on fear of a big giant black man, fear of his sexual might. Murray, this man understands that fear and love rule the world and if you can't get love, you'll get fear. I think people don't think so good when they are afraid."

As a classroom, we shifted our focus away from the text as a traditional "primary text" to primary texts that require more critical interpretation. We read interviews of political consultants who argued that reality did not impede their ability to weave plausible illusions. We read interviews with consultants who argued that commodities and candidates are sold in precisely the same way. Imagine the reaction of students who read that the goal of an advertising agency is to look "for better ways to convince our target viewer that if he drinks our beer, he'll get a better hard-on. It had nothing to do with our product . . . if they can make us get a hard-on, they can do anything with us."

These interviews, and primary sources in general, evoke strong and often prophetic insights from students because they are unedited, spontaneous, the memory of men and women who made the history our students study.

These interviews led my students to ask serious questions about what teachers usually call civics. They were not questions about separation of powers, or checks and balances, or the federal system—the standard fare of civics courses. The interviews, our primary sources, introduced us to real questions of American politics: the question of power and powerlessness, the question of illusion and reality. The interviews led us to issues of political alienation, questions of manipulation and deceit, the uses of racism in politics, the power of money in elections, and the creation and exploitation of anxiety. Tape recordings, interviews, diaries, correspondence, speeches, and films introduced us to reality. I urge teachers to use primary sources, which are plentiful and relatively easy to access on the Internet. They can provide students with a feeling for the nuance and the ambiguity of history—a sense of how difficult it is to interpret wisely. Students can interpret materials for themselves, dispute one another's conclusions—actually develop a feeling for the historian's craft. Many universities, foundations, and the Library of Congress have been recording oral histories for decades, copies of which are available and reasonably priced. Yale University and Steven Spielberg are sponsoring oral histories of Holocaust victims. Ask your school librarian to compile a list of available oral histories.

The ultimate primary source is autobiography. You should urge your students to maintain a journal. Every student has a story. The pain might be hidden but operative. Autobiography can be an invitation to bond, a cry for help, or a startling way to resolve conflict. Teachers might suggest that students write letters to their journal they know will never be sent. The unsent letter could be a fruitful way to express repressed anger or love or pain—a powerful catharsis—a significant step toward realizing who one is. Students could include important letters they have sent or received and articles, photographs, and quotes from newspapers and magazines that greatly affected them. They can draw in their journals or write poems or prayers. Teachers must guarantee privacy but welcome the desire to share.[7]

At the turn of the millennium, great teachers of social science and literature must concentrate on great issues and take risks. Abandoning textbooks for primary sources can be risky. Certainly it involves much more preparation. Innovative lesson plans that challenge prevailing assumptions can be very risky. Schools must deal with reality, and this can be done only by developing courses that pierce the veil of illusion, courses that deal with the power of the media, the insinuation and majesty of images in advertising, the creation of a one-dimensional language that stifles discordant views, and courses that demonstrate that the major political parties are barely distinguishable. Students must have opportunities to discuss their satisfaction or alienation.

Teachers must take risks. They must discuss the fragility of democracy and delineate the forces that transform democratic societies into plutocracies. Teachers who can help students distinguish illusion from reality may have prepared them to confront the real world, as skeptics, and hopefully as activists.

UNFINISHED NOTES ON PLANS FOR A GLOBAL HIGH SCHOOL: CURRICULUM AND GOALS

The global high school is designed to get young people to think about the most important questions of our time in ways that will develop their social consciousness and make them active citizens, not merely of a particular nation or culture but of the world, sensitive to the varieties of cultures. We examine the fragility of civil society and democracy and the aggressive forces that demand unlimited power and tyranny. We offer courses that illuminate humankind's need to create things of beauty and be poetic in the literal sense as well as courses that prepare students for practical action. We study how and why men and women try to understand the world through magic, science, and religion. We try to understand the causes of war and the conditions of peace. We examine violent and nonviolent means of social change. We explore the conflict between economic priorities and environmental safety. We are concerned with the roots of racism and nationalism. We study the causes of political alienation, the delegitimation of states, and the means for restoring popular power and democracy.

Our curriculum stresses the efforts of theorists to understand human aggression and our capacity for caring. We explore efforts to construct a social order that balances repression and freedom. We provide education centered on the recognition of patterns and structure. Because we are interested in potential and realization, we explore the process by which the past shapes the present and the future.

We study public health and human rights. We study those moments that make transcendence possible in science and art. We study why the wars of the next century are likely to be not between nations but between ethnic, religious, and racial groups. Our courses are designed to help students understand the complexity of globalism and feel empowered.

A large percentage of high school students in the United States believe they have no power whatsoever to alter society. The political alienation of students around the world is profound, and the legitimacy of states is questioned by millions of young people. We want our students to understand why this alienation and delegitimation is accelerating.

The ability to understand multiplicity should create students who

feel more competent and are more willing to make a personal investment in the well-being of others. Social responsibility and activism
are core elements of our curriculum and the culture of our schools.
This is why we embrace values that enhance empowerment, coopera-
tion, compassion, and respect.

Students must demonstrate their ability to model, to predict, to
replicate, and to convey their knowledge—sometimes in a public
forum—to others with clarity. On two occasions during the school
year, small groups of students will design experiments in science or
social science with the aid of teachers and present their findings, first
to fellow students and then to an audience of experts. These public
performances celebrate scholarship, discipline, and achievement. They
are a critical element in the creation of a meaningful school community.

Courses are designed to acquaint students with systems dynamics
so that their work will be integrative and generative. We hope to transcend the compartmentalization of knowledge, the common high
school approach that often produces poor results. We are interested
in comparative studies and chronology. These skills are helpful for
students who wish to create social change and, in turn, change themselves.

POTENTIAL SEMESTER COURSES FOR THE GLOBAL
HIGH SCHOOL

Dr. Charles Deutsch of the Harvard Project for Schooling and
Children developed a course titled "Global Disease and Community
Health: Research Skills for Health Activism," which serves as a good
example of what a course within the global high school would seek to
achieve. Deutsch designed the course to motivate students to become

activists in public health and to train them to deal with multiple causation and a wide range of possible effects. He trained four teachers
in the fundamental principles of epidemiology and medical statistics.[8]
Along with their students, these teachers, who specialized in math,
history, science, and literature, analyzed the causes and effects of four
major epidemics—cholera, polio, breast cancer, and AIDS—and
traced their impact on public-health systems, demographics, class, and
politics. The students also were trained in the fundamentals of medical statistics so that they could design and execute a serious research
project dealing with some aspect of public health.

The course forced students to recognize and statistically demonstrate the systemic nature of epidemics—the network of infection, the
panic, the diagnosis, the precautions, and the ebb and flow of illness
among social classes. They had to distinguish the economic and social
forces that could be accommodated only by change and those that
resisted change. Their ability to think and act as health activists de-
pended on whether they could apply what they learned about the
dynamics of one epidemic to other epidemics. Much of the beauty
and subtlety of this course was inherent in the process by which students understood that more effective ways of dealing with epidemics
necessitated significant changes in the distribution of health care,
medical education, and politics. The highly personal message implicit
in this work was that being a health activist is satisfying and challenging.

Dr. Deutsch's efforts demonstrate the systemic and dynamic quality of the platonic pedagogy. Prompting this ability to make connections, to anticipate reverberations between systems, is fundamental to
the pedagogy developed at Egleston Square. I audited several classes
and realized that Deutsch's course and those I taught at Egleston
could be refined and used as the basis for a radically different high

school—*the global high school*—designed to train socially active and responsible students by exposing them to global issues that might be catastrophic or enormously beneficial to society.

Democratic Theory and Its Critics

What is democratic theory? Why do politics in many "democratic" nations fail to meet the requirements of theory? What were the arguments against democracy in the eighteenth and twentieth centuries? What are the arguments offered now by alienated voters throughout the world who feel powerless?

What Is the Difference between Science, Magic, and Religion?

What is the scientific method? What are the essence and appeal of magic and religion, and how do they differ from science? What are the social, economic, and political conditions that set the stage for great advances in science? Despite the power of science, millions remain faithful to their gods or magic. We examine why this duality exists.

Is Peace Merely an Interlude between Wars?

Is war inevitable because aggression and survival are integral elements of human nature? Does war arise out of specific social-political-economic circumstances in which "war fever" is manufactured by elites or charismatic leaders before it spreads to the public. We examine the practice of using war to sustain power; unify nations; expand territory; acquire natural resources; provide outlets for ethnic, social, and religious antagonism; and alter the balance of power. We also are concerned with the conditions that promote long-term peace: mutual deterrence, international economic prosperity, and democratic and humanitarian values.

Comparative Economic Systems

We should conduct a comparative study of how economic problems are resolved under alternative economic systems and examine the theory and practice of various forms of capitalism, common property, utopianism, Marxism, central planning, market socialism, and worker self-management.

Freedom Is Fragile: Tyranny Is Brutal and Unforgiving

The twentieth century produced three massive tyrannies: Stalin's Russia, Hitler's Germany, and Mao's China. Does tyranny depend on a tradition of terror and militarism or prolonged economic distress or charismatic leaders? Can tyranny emerge in nations with a tradition of human rights? Is tyranny the only means of modernizing quickly? How did apocalyptic and conspiratorial theories as well as paranoid style become integral elements of the infrastructure of tyranny?

The Politics of Protest

Who protests? How do leaders recruit followers? What determines whether a movement is violent or nonviolent, successful or unsuccessful? Why do poor people's movements usually fail? We examine the suffrage movement, the struggle to organize labor, the civil rights movement, the anti-Vietnam protest in America, and protest movements in Mexico designed to dismantle feudalism and establish self-rule and democracy.

NOTES

1. I strongly recommend *Teaching for Understanding: Linking Research with Practice*, edited by Martha Stone Wiske (Jossey-Bass Publishers, 1998), a wise book that stresses the need to develop generative topics that resonate with the daily lives of students.

2. Bill Moyers, "Consuming Images: The Public Mind," PBS.

3. *Teach Me!* p. 120.

4. Herbert McClooky, "Consensus and Ideology in American Politics," *American Political Science Review*, 1964: vol. 58, pp. 361–382.

5. M. B. Levin, *The Alienated Voter, Politics in Boston*, Holt Rinehart and Winston, 1960. See also Levin and Eden, "Political Strategy for the Alienated Voter," *Public Opinion Quarterly*, vol. xxvi, no. 1, Spring 1963.

6. *Teach Me!* p. 62.

7. Conversations with Ruth Henderson, writer and doctoral candidate in narrative studies at the Union Institute, convinced me that autobiography can be a vital teaching tool.

8. The course was prepared for the Pilot School at Cambridge Ridge and Latin High School, Cambridge, Massachusetts.

About twenty students passed in and out of my courses during the three years I taught at Egleston. The young man who wanted to become a disc jockey is now attending Boston University at night. One of the young women who regularly attended class is a sophomore at the University of Massachusetts at Amherst. Robert and two of the "regulars" have completed their G.E.D. The one student I had who wanted to be a policewoman is now among Boston's finest. Two students who took "First Person History" attend Roxbury Community College, where they are doing well. One young woman attends a junior college in Florida.

One of my students, who appeared and disappeared from class with regularity, passed the state examination and is now a licensed specialist in heating and air conditioning. Another former student who had great difficulty paying attention in class is now a licensed dental assistant. Two students have become parents. One plans to complete junior college once she has earned enough money to pay the tuition; the other has decided not to attend college.

Of my two most thoughtful and innovative students, one has a serious drinking problem, and both work in retail sales and have no plans to continue their education. The student who loved to role-play Khrushchev apprenticed with his father and is now an auto mechanic.

As far as the school administration knows, none of these students have had any difficulty with the law. All are working, with the possible exception of three students who have not been heard from since graduation.